A Common Core Approach To Teaching
OF MICE AND MEN

Literature Lesson Plans

Written To The Common Core Standards

Teacher's Pet Publications

Copyright 2014

COPYRIGHT INFORMATION

This is copyrighted material.
It may not be copied or distributed in any way
without written permission from Teacher's Pet Publications.

The purchaser may copy the student materials
for his or her classroom use only.
No other portion may be copied or distributed in any way.

No portion may be posted on the Internet
without written permission from Teacher's Pet Publications.

Copyright violations are prosecuted to the fullest extent of the law
and are subject to a minimum of a $500.00 fine,
imposed by Teacher's Pet Publications,
in addition to any other legal judgments obtained.

Copyright questions?
Contact Teacher's Pet Publications
www.tpet.com
1-800-255-8935

ISBN
978-1-60249-504-3
Copyright 2014

Teacher's Pet Publications
11504 Hammock Point Road
Berlin, Maryland 21811
www.tpet.com

Table Of Contents

Chapter 1
    Reading Activity 1: True or False 7
    Reading Activity 2: Analyzing Passages 14
    Reading Activity 3: Characters, Lexicon, & Diction 21
    Reading Activity 4: Action, Character, Decision 26
    Reading Activity 5: Figurative Language 29
    Reading Activity 6: Elements of Fiction & Literary Devices 32
    Reading Activity 7: Meaning And Inferences 38
    Writing Activity 1: What Is Friendship 45
    Suggested Writing Assignments 49
    Quick-Write Assignments 51

Chapter 2
    Reading Activity 1: True or False 55
    Reading Activity 2: Analyzing Passages 61
    Reading Activity 3: Physical Attributes & Characterization 68
    Reading Activity 4: Action, Character, Decision 72
    Reading Activity 5: Figurative Language 75
    Reading Activity 6: Elements of Fiction & Literary Devices 78
    Reading Activity 7: Meaning And Inferences 83
    Writing Activity 1: What Is Masculinity? 90
    Suggested Writing Assignments 95
    Quick-Write Assignments 97

Chapter 3
    Reading Activity 1: True or False 101
    Reading Activity 2: Analyzing Passages 108
    Reading Activity 3: Foil Character Study 113
    Reading Activity 4: Action, Character, Decision 116
    Reading Activity 5: Figurative Language 119
    Reading Activity 6: Elements of Fiction & Literary Devices 122
    Reading Activity 7: Meaning And Inferences 127
    Writing Activity 1: How Is Weakness Or Strength Determined? 135
    Suggested Writing Assignments 140
    Quick-Write Assignments 142

Chapter 4
    Reading Activity 1: True or False 145
    Reading Activity 2: Analyzing Passages 152
    Reading Activity 3: Direct vs. Indirect Characterization 158
    Reading Activity 4: Action, Character, Decision 161
    Reading Activity 5: Figurative Language 164
    Reading Activity 6: Elements of Fiction & Literary Devices 167
    Reading Activity 7: Meaning And Inferences 172
    Writing Activity 1: What Are The Effects Of Isolation? 179
    Suggested Writing Assignments 183
    Quick-Write Assignments 185

Table Of Contents, Continued

Chapter 5
    Reading Activity 1: True or False   189
    Reading Activity 2: Analyzing Passages   196
    Reading Activity 3: Round Characters or Stereotypes?   202
    Reading Activity 4: Action, Character, Decision   206
    Reading Activity 5: Figurative Language   209
    Reading Activity 6: Elements of Fiction & Literary Devices   212
    Reading Activity 7: Meaning And Inferences   217
    Writing Activity 1: What Does Curley's Wife Symbolize?   222
    Suggested Writing Assignments   226
    Quick-Write Assignments   228

Chapter 6
    Reading Activity 1: True or False   231
    Reading Activity 2: Analyzing Passages   238
    Reading Activity 3: A Closer Look At Lennie   244
    Reading Activity 4: Action, Character, Decision   247
    Reading Activity 5: Figurative Language   250
    Reading Activity 6: Elements of Fiction & Literary Devices   253
    Reading Activity 7: Meaning And Inferences   258
    Writing Activity 1: Is Murder An Act of Friendship?   265
    Suggested Writing Assignments   269
    Quick-Write Assignments   271

Overview
    Reading Activity 1: True or False   275
    Reading Activity 2: Analyzing Passages   282
    Reading Activity 3: Characters, Motivation, & Dreams   288
    Reading Activity 4: Action, Character, Decision   292
    Reading Activity 5: Figurative Language   295
    Reading Activity 6: Elements of Fiction & Literary Devices   298
    Reading Activity 7: Meaning And Inferences   301
    Writing Activity 1: Sharing A Common Dream   308
    Suggested Writing Assignments   312
    Quick-Write Assignments   314

MATERIALS: CHAPTER 1
OF MICE AND MEN

Reading Activity 1: True or False?

Reading Activity 2: Analyzing Passages

Reading Activity 3: Characters, Lexicon, and Diction

Reading Activity 4: Action, Character, Decision

Reading Activity 5: Figurative Language

Reading Activity 6: Elements of Fiction & Literary Devices

Reading Activity 7: Meaning and Inferences

Writing Activity 1: What Is Friendship?

Suggested Writing Assignments

Quick-Write Assignments

NOTES
OF MICE AND MEN

Of Mice And Men Chapter 1
Reading Activity 1: True or False?

Anchor Standard	8th Grade	9th-10th Grade
CCRA.R.1	RL.8.1	RL.9-10.1
CCRA.SL.1	SL.8.1	SL.9-10.1
CCRA.SL.4	SL.8.4	SL.9-10.4

Objectives
- Students will be able to cite the parts of the text that support their analysis of what the text says or infers.
- Students will consider statements about the text, determine whether those statements are true or false, and will give textual evidence supporting their choices.
- Students will work together in small groups to discuss, analyze, and evaluate the statements made.
- Students will evaluate the analytical work of their peers.

Directions

Prior to reading chapter 1: Give students (or post) the following list of statements about the chapters, and explain to students that they should read Chapter 1 to find out if these statements are true or false:

Lennie is not capable of traveling by himself.
Lennie lies, but he does not do it maliciously.
Lennie was believed to have attacked a woman in Weed.
Lennie believes that his dream is attainable.
George believes that Lennie's behavior will not cause another crisis.
George is more impatient with Lennie than he is patient and understanding.

After reading chapter 1: The worksheets on the following pages can be done by students individually, in small groups, or as a whole class. Below are directions to use the questions as a group activity to fulfill more state standards:

- Cut the worksheet apart, making each question and answer box a slip.
- Divide your class into six groups and give one question and a True/False evaluation form to each group. Tell students they are to discuss the statement and determine if the statement is true or false, supporting their decision with evidence from the text. Tell them their answers will be evaluated on the criteria given on the evaluation form.
- Give students ample time to discuss the statements and record their answers.
- Have the groups swap True or False question slips so that each group can evaluate another group's answer. The group should fill in the number of the question they are evaluating, decide how well the answer fulfills the criteria listed, and fill out the form accordingly.
- Repeat the previous step until all the groups have evaluated each others' answers.
- Collect the evaluations and answer slips.

Follow-Up/Assessment/Extension:

- You could average and record the grades each group received for its answers.
- Students could write in their journals or notebooks one thing they learned from this activity.
- You could hold a whole-class discussion about each or any of the statements, either solely orally or using a blank True or False Worksheet on your whiteboard, filling it in as the discussion unfolds.
- At the beginning of the next class, you could hold a brief discussion reviewing the facts addressed by the True/False Worksheet, to see what students have retained and to reinforce the information.
- You could have students make up (and fill in) their own True/False Worksheets for other information located within this chapter.

Of Mice And Men Chapter 1: True or False?

Write *True* or *False* in the blank next to each statement. Below the statement, explain why you chose true or false, referencing the text to support your choices.

_____ 1. Lennie is not capable of traveling by himself.

_____ 2. Lennie lies, but he does not do it maliciously.

_____ 3. Lennie was believed to have attacked a woman in Weed.

Of Mice And Men Chapter 1 True or False? Page 2

_____ 4. Lennie believes that his dream is attainable.

_____ 5. George believes that Lennie's behavior will not cause another crisis.

_____ 6. George is more impatient with Lennie than he is patient and understanding.

Of Mice And Men Chapter 1 True or False? Evaluation

List Your Group's Members: Your Group's Question # _____

_____   _____   _____

_____   _____   _____

1 = No, Not At All **2** = A Little **3** = Some **4** = Yes **5** = Yes, Very Well

Evaluation of Question # ___
Does the explanation support the answer of true or false?   1 2 3 4 5
Is there good textual evidence to support the answer?   1 2 3 4 5
Is the answer clearly stated?   1 2 3 4 5
                       Total Score _____ of a possible 15 points

Evaluation of Question # ___
Does the explanation support the answer of true or false?   1 2 3 4 5
Is there good textual evidence to support the answer?   1 2 3 4 5
Is the answer clearly stated?   1 2 3 4 5
                       Total Score _____ of a possible 15 points

Evaluation of Question # ___
Does the explanation support the answer of true or false?   1 2 3 4 5
Is there good textual evidence to support the answer?   1 2 3 4 5
Is the answer clearly stated?   1 2 3 4 5
                       Total Score _____ of a possible 15 points

Evaluation of Question # ___
Does the explanation support the answer of true or false?   1 2 3 4 5
Is there good textual evidence to support the answer?   1 2 3 4 5
Is the answer clearly stated?   1 2 3 4 5
                       Total Score _____ of a possible 15 points

Evaluation of Question # ___
Does the explanation support the answer of true or false?   1 2 3 4 5
Is there good textual evidence to support the answer?   1 2 3 4 5
Is the answer clearly stated?   1 2 3 4 5
                       Total Score _____ of a possible 15 points

Of Mice And Men Chapter 1: True or False? Suggested Answers

Write *True* or *False* in the blank next to each statement. Below the statement, explain why you chose true or false, referencing the text to support your choices.

<u>TRUE</u>   1. Lennie is not capable of traveling by himself.

> It is clear from very early on that George looks after Lennie and takes care of him. When George mentions work cards and bus tickets and Lennie thinks he's lost his, George responds by saying "'You never had none, you crazy bastard. I got both of 'em here. Think I'd let you carry your own work card?'". This quote demonstrates that Lennie is not capable of traveling by himself.

<u>TRUE</u>   2. Lennie lies, but he does not do it maliciously.

> Lennie does lie to George when he says his pocket is empty. When George notices Lennie's hand is in his pocket, he asks Lennie what he has and Lennie says "I ain't got nothin', George. Honest." However, we learn that this lie does not have any malicious intent behind it when he tells George "It's on'y a mouse […] [to] pet with my thumb while we walked along." Lennie only lies about having the mouse because he knows George will take it if he finds it; there is no sinister motive behind his lie.

<u>TRUE</u>   3. Lennie was believed to have attacked a woman in Weed.

> After George tells Lennie not to talk to the ranch boss, he says "An' you ain't gonna do no bad things like you done in Weed, neither." By saying this, the reader can infer that Lennie did something to get them chased out of Weed. Later, George confronts Lennie for what he did in Weed: "Well, how the hell did she know you jus' wanted to feel her dress? She jerks back and you hold on like it was a mouse." When George says this, the reader learns that Lennie's interaction with the woman was interpreted as an attack.

Of Mice And Men Chapter 1 True or False? Suggested Answers Page 2

<u>TRUE</u> 4. Lennie believes that his dream is attainable.

Lennie's dream is to own a small farm filled with rabbits with George. Lennie is so set on this dream that he has even memorized George's speech about it. When he starts reciting the speech with George, George says "Why'n't you do it yourself? You know all of it." (13) Lennie absolutely believes that this dream is attainable, which is clear when he says to George "Let's have different color rabbits." Lennie's daydreaming about specific details of the farm shows that he is convinced that this dream will come true.

<u>FALSE</u> 5. George believes that Lennie's behavior will not cause another crisis.

George does believe that Lennie could easily land the two of them in another crisis. Because of this, he tells Lennie: "If you jus' happen to get in trouble like you always done before, I want you to come right here an' hide in the brush." George's planning for what to do if Lennie does get in trouble again shows that he does not have faith that Lennie will stay out of trouble.

<u>FALSE</u> 6. George is more impatient with Lennie than he is patient and understanding.

George can get impatient with Lennie, and does when he explodes at Lennie for asking for ketchup with his beans. Lennie reacts to this by saying, "If you don' want me I can go off in the hills an' find a cave. I can go away any time." George quickly reacts to Lennie's statement and says, "No – look! I was jus' foolin', Lennie. 'Cause I want you to stay with me." This reaction shows that while he can be impatient with Lennie, he is generally patient and understanding.

Of Mice And Men Chapter 1
Reading Activity 2: Analyzing Passages

Anchor Standard	8th Grade	9th-10th Grade
CCRA.R.6	RL.8.1	RL.9-10.1
	RL.8.3	
	RL.8.4	RL.9-10.4
	RL.8.6	
CCRA.SL.1	SL.8.1	SL.9-10.1

Objectives
- Students will analyze what the text says explicitly as well as inferences drawn from the text.
- Students will analyze how different points of view of the characters and the audience (or reader) creates suspense or humor.
- Students will analyze the impact of specific word choices on meaning and tone.

Directions
On the pages that follow, there are 8 passages to analyze, each with a question or questions to guide the process. There are many ways to use these questions:

- You could use them as a worksheet for all students to complete individually.
- You could use the worksheet as your guide in a whole-class discussion. Have students turn to the first passage in the book, read it, then ask the question(s) orally. Repeat through all 8 questions.
- You could assign one passage to each of 8 different groups of students, for the students to discuss and come up with responses to the question(s). Then hold a whole-class discussion.
- You could read the passage and then see which student can find the passage first (to practice skimming skills). Then follow up with the questions(s) and discussion.
- You could have students choose one or two questions to respond to in writing in their notebooks or journals.

Follow-Up/Assessment/Extension
- Ask students to write about the dynamic between George and Lennie. Does George feel indignation or obligation? Does Lennie feel guilt or shame?
- Have students pick out other passages in this chapter that show interesting word usage, descriptions, or lack of clarity.
- As an introduction to this activity and this chapter, ask students to write about the responsibilities that friends have toward one another.

Of Mice And Men Chapter 1 Analyzing Passages

Answer the questions following the quotations completely.

1. "…[Lennie] walked heavily, dragging his feet a little, way a bear drags his paws. His arms did not swing at his sides, but hung loosely….Lennie dabbled his big paw in the water and wiggled his fingers so the water arose in little splashes; rings widened across the pool on the other side and came back again."

How is Lennie described physically? Why is it significant?

2. "What you want of a dead mouse, anyways?"
"I could pet it with my thumb while we walked along," said Lennie.

Why does Lennie want the mouse? How does he benefit from having it? What does this reveal about his judgment?

3. "[Lennie] said gently, "George… I ain't got mine. I musta lost it." He looked down at the ground in despair.

"You never had none, you crazy bastard. I got both of 'em here. Think I'd let you carry your own work card?"

Lennie grinned with relief.

How does this interchange characterize their relationship? How does "crazy bastard" contrast with George's care for Lennie?

Of Mice And Men Chapter 1 Analyzing Passages Page 2

4. "That ranch we're goin' to is right down there about a quarter mile. We're gonna go in an' see the boss. Now, look—I'll give him the work tickets, but you ain't gonna say a word. You jus' stand there and don't say nothing. If he finds out what a crazy bastard you are, we won't get no job, but if he sees ya work before he hears ya talk, we're set."

What does this suggest about Lennie's ability to work? How does that contrast with his ability to think?

5. "Lennie looked sadly up at him. "They was so little," he said apologetically. "I'd pet 'em, and pretty soon they bit my fingers and I pinched their heads a little and then they was dead— because they was so little. I wish't we'd get the rabbits pretty soon, George. They ain't so little."

Why is the repetition of the word "little" significant?

6. "Guys like us, that work on ranches, are the loneliest guys in the world. They got no family. They don't belong no place. They come to a ranch an' work up a stake and then they go inta town and blow their stake, and the first thing you know they're poundin' their tail on some other ranch. They ain't got nothing to look ahead to."

Is George lonely? Does he contradict himself?

7. "[George] heard Lennie's whimpering cry and wheeled about. "Blubberin' like a baby! Jesus Christ! A big guy like you!" Lennie's lip quivered and tears started in his eyes. "Aw, Lennie!" George put his hand on Lennie's shoulder. "I ain't takin' it away jus' for meanness. That mouse ain't fresh, Lennie; and besides, you've broke it pettin' it. You get another mouse that's fresh and I'll let you keep it a little while."

Consider the word "big." How is it ironic?

8. "I wish I could put you in a cage with about a million mice an' let you have fun." His anger left him suddenly. He looked across the fire at Lennie's anguished face, and then he looked ashamedly at the flames."

What does this suggest about George's attitude toward Lennie?

Of Mice And Men Chapter 1 Analyzing Passages Suggested Answers

Answer the questions following the quotations completely.

1. "…[Lennie] walked heavily, dragging his feet a little, way a bear drags his paws. His arms did not swing at his sides, but hung loosely….Lennie dabbled his big paw in the water and wiggled his fingers so the water arose in little splashes; rings widened across the pool on the other side and came back again."

How is Lennie described physically? Why is it significant?
Lennie's physical features are described as analogous to a bear's features. His hand is called a "paw," and his gait is described as similar to a bear's. The description of his physical features is very animal-like. This is significant because Lennie consequently appears to the reader as animal-like, and less human. He is also connected to the natural world, which is central to the setting in the Eden-like farmland of California.

2. "What you want of a dead mouse, anyways?"
"I could pet it with my thumb while we walked along," said Lennie.

Why does Lennie want the mouse? How does he benefit from having it? What does this reveal about his judgment?
Lennie wants the mouse because he is comforted by petting it. He likes the feel of petting fur (which is clear when George mentions Lennie's rejection of a rubber mouse from Aunt Clara), so he keeps the dead mouse in his pocket so that he can pet the mouse's fur. However, the mouse is not fresh, and is broken from Lennie petting it. Lennie's ignorance of these two facts shows that he does not have good judgment at all, and that his desire for tactile things is stronger than common sense (to dispose of a rotting animal corpse).

3. "[Lennie] said gently, "George… I ain't got mine. I musta lost it." He looked down at the ground in despair.
"You never had none, you crazy bastard. I got both of 'em here. Think I'd let you carry your own work card?"
Lennie grinned with relief.

How does this interchange characterize their relationship? How does "crazy bastard" appear to contrast with George's care for Lennie?
This quote solidifies George's role in relation to Lennie as that of a caregiver. By holding on to Lennie's work card and bus ticket, George makes it clear that he not only recognizes Lennie's need for someone to look after him, but also that he has taken on that responsibility himself. George calling Lennie a "crazy bastard" is in contrast to the gentleness and care with which George gives Lennie. Rather than using the name "crazy bastard" as an insult or an attack on Lennie, George uses that as an affectionate nickname when he is frustrated by Lennie.

Of Mice And Men Chapter 1 Analyzing Passages Suggested Answers Page 2

4. "That ranch we're goin' to is right down there about a quarter mile. We're gonna go in an' see the boss. Now, look—I'll give him the work tickets, but you ain't gonna say a word. You jus' stand there and don't say nothing. If he finds out what a crazy bastard you are, we won't get no job, but if he sees ya work before he hears ya talk, we're set."

What does this suggest about Lennie's ability to work? How does that contrast with his ability to think?
George's implication that Lennie should let his work speak for himself suggests that Lennie is an incredibly good worker, and that his ability to work makes up for his mental slowness. The work that Lennie would be doing on a farm would presumably be physical labor, so George suggests that Lennie is very strong. However, it is clear that Lennie is not smart at all, so this quote serves to set up the clear gap between Lennie's physical strength and his mental strength.

5. "Lennie looked sadly up at him. "They was so little," he said apologetically. "I'd pet 'em, and pretty soon they bit my fingers and I pinched their heads a little and then they was dead—because they was so little. I wish't we'd get the rabbits pretty soon, George. They ain't so little."

Why is the repetition of the word "little" significant?
Lennie's repetition of the word "little" is significant for a few reasons. First of all, it shows Lennie's strength. In Lennie's eyes, he would barely do anything to the mice, merely "pinching their heads a little," but that was enough to kill them. Secondly, the repetition shows that he does not think of the lives of the mice as important. He killed mouse after mouse "because they was so little," but continued to do it regardless. The word also connects to Lennie, whose last name is, ironically, "Small."

6. "Guys like us, that work on ranches, are the loneliest guys in the world. They got no family. They don't belong no place. They come to a ranch an' work up a stake and then they go inta town and blow their stake, and the first thing you know they're poundin' their tail on some other ranch. They ain't got nothing to look ahead to."

Is George lonely? Does he contradict himself?
George describes the life of a rancher as incredibly lonely. According to him, they have no family, no home, and nothing to work towards. But George's life is not lonely (despite being a rancher himself) because he has Lennie and he and Lennie have plans to look forward to. In George's words, "With us it ain't like that. We got a future. We got somebody to talk to that gives a damn about us." (13) George does contradict himself therefore because despite living a rancher's life, he is not lonely.

Of Mice And Men Chapter 1 Analyzing Passages Suggested Answers Page 3

7. "[George] heard Lennie's whimpering cry and wheeled about. "Blubberin' like a baby! Jesus Christ! A big guy like you!" Lennie's lip quivered and tears started in his eyes. "Aw, Lennie!" George put his hand on Lennie's shoulder. "I ain't takin' it away jus' for meanness. That mouse ain't fresh, Lennie; and besides, you've broke it pettin' it. You get another mouse that's fresh and I'll let you keep it a little while."

Consider the word "big." How is it ironic?
The word "big" is ironic because while Lennie has been described as animal-like and incredibly strong, he is crying due to something as childish as his dead mouse being taken away. Even though Lennie is physically big, he is emotionally not big. His physical size does not match his maturity level because while he is physically big, he has the maturity of a small child. Also, there is irony in that Lennie's last name is Small.

8. "I wish I could put you in a cage with about a million mice an' let you have fun." His anger left him suddenly. He looked across the fire at Lennie's anguished face, and then he looked ashamedly at the flames."

What does this suggest about George's attitude toward Lennie?
George's shame and embarrassment for lashing out at Lennie suggests that while Lennie can make George impatient, George cares very much for Lennie. George is clearly very sensitive to the fact that he may have hurt Lennie's feelings, and because of this he worries about what Lennie's reaction to his hurtful words will be. George is clearly very affectionate towards Lennie, despite his short temper with him.

Of Mice And Men Chapter 1
Reading Activity 3: Characters, Lexicon and Diction

Anchor Standard	8th Grade	9th-10th Grade
CCRA.R.1	RL.8.1	RL.9-10.1
CCRA.SL.1	SL.8.1	SL.9-10.1

Objectives
Using textual evidence, students will explore how characterization is created through the use of different levels of lexicon and diction.

Directions
The characters, lexicon and diction worksheet on the following page could be used in many ways, completed by small groups of students, individual students, or as a whole class activity.

Students will be able to identify how different levels of lexicon and diction create characterization. Students can use their current observations about the characters' lexicon and diction to understand characteristics and qualities associated with the main two characters.

Students may (and should) use their books to skim through the chapter to refresh their memories or gather more information about the characters.

After students complete the worksheets discuss students' answers as a whole class. Collect the worksheets for grading, if you choose, or have students put them in their notebooks for further study.

Follow-Up/Assessment/Extension
Revisit this assignment later in the unit and discuss the how differences (social class and race for example) are conveyed through diction and lexicon.

Of Mice And Men Chapter 1
Reading Activity 3: Characters, Lexicon and Diction

Authors have many tools for creating characterization. Among those tools are lexicon, the words characters speak, and diction, the way characters use words to express themselves. These authorial choices affect the way readers perceive and understand characters and their motivations.

Complete the chart below, focusing on the lexicon and diction of Lennie and George. Go back and skim the text if you need to, to refresh your memory about these characters.

Speaker & Quote	Comment on the character's lexicon. (Does it convey ignorance, intelligence? Is it grammatical? Be specific.)	Comment on the character's diction. (Is it direct? Is it confident? Hesitant? Evasive? Be specific.)	What do your observations about lexicon and diction suggest about the speaker?
George: "Tastes all right," he admitted. "Don't really seem to be running, though. You never oughta drink water when it ain't running, Lennie," he said hopelessly. "You'd drink out of a gutter if you was thirsty."			
George: "Aw, Lennie!" George put his hand on Lennie's shoulder. "I ain't takin' it away jus' for meanness. That mouse ain't fresh, Lennie; and besides, you've broke it pettin' it. You get another mouse that's fresh and I'll let you keep it a little while."			

Of Mice And Men Chapter 1 Reading Activity 3: Characters, Lexicon and Diction Page 2

Speaker & Quote	Comment on the character's lexicon. (Does it convey ignorance, intelligence? Is it grammatical? Be specific.)	Comment on the character's diction. (Is it direct? Is it confident? Hesitant? Evasive? Be specific.)	What do your observations about lexicon and diction suggest about the speaker?
Lennie: "I was only foolin', George. I don't want no ketchup. I wouldn't eat no ketchup if it was right here beside me."			
Lennie: "An' live off the fatta the lan'," Lennie shouted. "An' have rabbits. Go on, George! Tell about what we're gonna have in the garden and about the rabbits in the cages and about the rain in the winter and the stove, and how thick the cream is on the milk like you can hardly cut it. Tell about that, George."			

Of Mice And Men Chapter 1
Reading Activity 3: Characters, Lexicon and Diction Suggested Answers

Authors have many tools for creating characterization. Among those tools are lexicon, the words characters speak, and diction, the way characters use words to express themselves. These authorial choices affect the way readers perceive and understand characters and their motivations.

Complete the chart below, focusing on the lexicon and diction of Lennie and George. Go back and skim the text if you need to, to refresh your memory about these characters.

Speaker & Quote	Comment on the character's lexicon. (Does it convey ignorance, intelligence? Is it grammatical? Be specific.)	Comment on the character's diction. (Is it direct? Is it confident? Hesitant? Evasive? Be specific.)	What do your observations about lexicon and diction suggest about the speaker?
George: "Tastes all right," he admitted. "Don't really seem to be running, though. You never oughta drink water when it ain't running, Lennie," he said hopelessly. "You'd drink out of a gutter if you was thirsty."	George has a very informal and colloquial manner of speaking, as is shown by his slang, improper grammar, and abbreviations. However, he is also clearly intelligent despite the grammar mistakes, as is seen by his knowledge of safe drinking water.	George's diction is quite straightforward, as is seen by his simple sentences when he talks to Lennie. He does not use frivolous words to convey what he wants to say, but rather merely states it.	These observations suggest that George is a simple, rugged man who is not concerned with other people's opinions of him. They also suggest that while he may not be "book-smart", George is "street-smart".
George: "Aw, Lennie!" George put his hand on Lennie's shoulder. "I ain't takin' it away jus' for meanness. That mouse ain't fresh, Lennie; and besides, you've broke it pettin' it. You get another mouse that's fresh and I'll let you keep it a little while."	In this quote, George speaks again with colloquial language that contains improper grammar. The repetition of slang and abbreviations show that George has a very rural and unschooled style of speaking.	George's diction is comforting and consoling in this quote. This is seen in his attempts to make Lennie understand and feel better about him taking away the dead mouse.	This quote reaffirms George's role of caretaker to Lennie. This role is seen in the care he takes in using diction to comfort Lennie when he is distraught. This caring demeanor is contrasted by George's rough and uncultured lexicon.

Of Mice And Men Chapter 1 Reading Activity 3: Characters, Lexicon and Diction Suggested Answers Page 2

Speaker & Quote	Comment on the character's lexicon. (Does it convey ignorance, intelligence? Is it grammatical? Be specific.)	Comment on the character's diction. (Is it direct? Is it confident? Hesitant? Evasive? Be specific.)	What do your observations about lexicon and diction suggest about the speaker?
Lennie: "I was only foolin', George. I don't want no ketchup. I wouldn't eat no ketchup if it was right here beside me."	Lennie speaks with very improper grammar, as is seen by his confused sentence structure. This serves to flesh out his slow-mindedness.	In this quote, Lennie's diction is apologetic and submissive, as is seen by his repeated attempts to make George understand his sorrow for wanting ketchup.	Lennie's lexicon and diction in this quote suggest that he looks up to George, and accepts him as his leader.
Lennie: "An' live off the fatta the lan'," Lennie shouted. "An' have rabbits. Go on, George! Tell about what we're gonna have in the garden and about the rabbits in the cages and about the rain in the winter and the stove, and how thick the cream is on the milk like you can hardly cut it. Tell about that, George."	Lennie continues to use improper grammar and speaks in run-on sentences in this quote. This conveys rushed way of talking conveys excitement.	Lennie's diction is enthusiastic and hopeful. This mirrors his attitude when he thinks about his future on the farm, which is one of joy and hopefulness of success.	Lennie's run-on sentences and rushed grammar display his excitement because it shows that he can't stop talking about the future.

Of Mice And Men Chapter 1
Reading Activity 4: Action, Character, Decision

Anchor Standard	8th Grade	9th-10th Grade
CCRA.R.1	RL.8.3	
CCRA.SL.1	SL.8.1	SL.9-10.1

Objective
Students will identify whether particular lines of dialogue or incidents in the story propel the action, reveal aspects of a character, or provoke a decision

Directions
The following page contains passages from Chapter 1 of Of Mice and Men. Students should determine whether the passages advance the action, reveal aspects of a character, or provoke a decision.
This can be done as a whole-class activity, individually, or in small groups.

Follow-Up/Assessment/Extension
Have students skim Chapter 1 to find one example of a passage that propels the action, one that reveals aspects of a character, and one that provokes a decision. Again, this could be done individually or as a group.

Of Mice And Men Chapter 1: Action, Character, Decision

Write **A** (for Action) **C** (for Character) or **D** (for Decision) in the blank next to each to identify whether the passage/statement advances the action, tells us more about a character, or provokes a decision. On the lines under each question, provide a short explanation of your choice.

____ 1. Lennie dabbled his big paw in the water and wiggled his fingers so the water arose in little splashes; rings widened across the pool to the other side and came back again. Lennie watched them go. "Look, George. Look what I done."

____ 2. "Ain't a thing in my pocket," Lennie said cleverly.

____ 3. "God, you're a lot of trouble," said George. "I could get along so easy and so nice if I didn't have you on my tail. I could live so easy and maybe have a girl."

____ 4. George's hand remained outstretched imperiously. Slowly, like a terrier who doesn't want to bring a ball to its master, Lennie approached, drew back, approached again. George snapped his fingers sharply, and at the sound Lennie laid the mouse in his hand.

____ 5. "Tell you what I'll do, Lennie. First chance I get I'll give you a pup. Maybe you wouldn't kill it. That'd be better than mice. And you could pet it harder."

Of Mice And Men Chapter 1:
Action, Character, Decision Suggested Answers

Write **A** (for Action) **C** (for Character) or **D** (for Decision) in the blank next to each to identify whether the passage/statement advances the action, tells us more about a character, or provokes a decision. On the lines under each question, provide a short explanation of your choice.

C 1. Lennie dabbled his big paw in the water and wiggled his fingers so the water arose in little splashes; rings widened across the pool to the other side and came back again. Lennie watched them go. "Look, George. Look what I done."
This passage reveals Lennie's simplicity and the joy he finds in tactile things that preoccupy him. The water and the word "paw" connect Lennie to the natural world, depicting him as animal-like, which could depict him as unburdened by many of the the problems that plague humans.

A 2. "Ain't a thing in my pocket," Lennie said cleverly.
The lie that Lennie tells about carrying the dead mouse sparks conflict between George and Lennie, and it is conflict which move a narrative forward. We see the dynamics of their relationship as a result of Lennie's lie. George is strict and domineering and Lennie is submissive and sorrowful, yet George has genuine care for Lennie and a deep sense of responsibility for him. All of this conflict—between what George instructs Lennie to do and what Lennie actually does—fuels the story and its eventual resolution.

A 3. "God, you're a lot of trouble," said George. "I could get along so easy and so nice if I didn't have you on my tail. I could live so easy and maybe have a girl."
This statement is only partially true, as it is clear that George benefits from Lennie's companionship. However, it does reveal an important internal conflict that moves the story forward, as George himself and others questions his motives and why he would want to be burdened by Lennie.

D 4. George's hand remained outstretched imperiously. Slowly, like a terrier who doesn't want to bring a ball to its master, Lennie approached, drew back, approached again. George snapped his fingers sharply, and at the sound Lennie laid the mouse in his hand.
Lennie resists George's parental directives, but is ultimately compelled to make the decision himself to comply with George's authority.

D 5. "Tell you what I'll do, Lennie. First chance I get I'll give you a pup. Maybe you wouldn't kill it. That'd be better than mice. And you could pet it harder."
George makes a decision that Lennie can be responsible for keeping a pup alive. Later in the novel, this decision turns out to have important and fatal unintended consequences.

Of Mice And Men Chapter 1
Reading Activity 5: Figurative Language

Anchor Standard	8th Grade	9th-10th Grade
CCRA.R.4	RL.8.4	RL.9-10.4
CCRA.SL.1	SL.8.1	SL.9-10.1

Objectives
- Students will determine the meaning of words and phrases as they are used in the text, including figurative and connotative meanings.
- Students will determine how figurative language contributes to meaning.

Directions
The following page has a passage from the text which includes examples of figurative language. This work-sheet can be done individually, as a whole-class activity, or in small groups. Discuss the answers as a whole class. Collect the worksheets and record the grades if you choose to do so.

Follow-Up/Assessment/Extension
Ask students to begin tracking instances of a particular type of figurative language (personification, metaphor, hyperbole, etc.) in the text. Ask students to make a list to track their observations. Assign students a paper that uses these examples to make an argument about how the language creates meaning.

Of Mice And Men Chapter 1: Figurative Language

Read the following passages and determine if the passage contains a metaphor (M), simile (S) or no figurative language (NF). On the lines below, explain how the similes or metaphors create meaning in the passage.

_____1. On the sand banks the rabbits sat as quietly as little gray sculptured stones.

_____2. Behind him walked his opposite, a huge man, shapeless of face, with large, pale eyes, and wide, sloping shoulders; and he walked heavily, dragging his feet a little, the way a bear drags his paws. His arms did not swing at his sides, but hung loosely.

_____3. His huge companion dropped his blankets and flung himself down and drank from the surface of the green pool; drank with long gulps, snorting into the water like a horse.

_____4. Lennie hesitated, backed away, looked wildly at the brush line as though he contemplated running for his freedom.

_____5. "Blubberin' like a baby! Jesus Christ! A big guy like you."

Of Mice And Men Chapter 1: Figurative Language Suggested Answers

Read the following passages and determine if the passage contains a metaphor (M), simile (S) or no figurative language (NF). On the lines below, explain how the similes or metaphors create meaning in the passage.

S 1. On the sand banks the rabbits sat as quietly as little gray sculptured stones.
This quote is a simile because it says the rabbits sat "as quietly as" little gray sculptured stones. This simile compares rabbits to stones with the use of the word "as."

M 2. Behind him walked his opposite, a huge man, shapeless of face, with large, pale eyes, and wide, sloping shoulders; and he walked heavily, dragging his feet a little, the way a bear drags his paws. His arms did not swing at his sides, but hung loosely.
This quote is a metaphor because it described this man (Lennie) as if he were a bear, but does not set his description up in comparison to a bear.

S 3. His huge companion dropped his blankets and flung himself down and drank from the surface of the green pool; drank with long gulps, snorting into the water like a horse.
This quote is a simile because the way he drinks water is compared to a horse with the word "like."

NF 4. Lennie hesitated, backed away, looked wildly at the brush line as though he contemplated running for his freedom.
No figurative language.

S 5. "Blubberin' like a baby! Jesus Christ! A big guy like you."
This quote is a simile because his crying is compared to the way a baby cries with the word "like."

Of Mice And Men Chapter 1
Reading Activity 6: Elements of Fiction & Literary Devices

Anchor Standard	8th Grade	9th-10th Grade
CCRA.R.1	RL.8.1	RL.9-10.1
	RL.8.2	RL.9-10.2
	RL.8.3	RL.9-10.4
	RL.8.4	RL.9-10.5
	RL.8.6	
CCRA.SL.1	SL.8.1	SL.9-10.1

Objective
Students will study and discuss passages from the text to examine symbol, motif and theme and explore how these create meaning in the text.

Directions
Use the following discussion questions as a guide to discussing symbol, motif and theme, in these chapters.

You can give students the questions ahead of time and have them formulate answers prior to the class discussion or you can jump right in with a whole class discussion without student preparation if your students will handle that well.

As you hold the class discussion, be sure to include conversations defining symbol, motif and theme and explaining how these work together to advance meaning in the text.

Follow-Up/Assessment/Extension
After your discussion, ask students to look for recurrences of these symbols, motifs and themes in future chapters.

Of Mice And Men Chapter 1: Elements of Fiction & Literary Devices

One of the primary motifs in the novel is rabbits. Consider the following passages and what meaning the references to rabbits creates in the novel.

1. On the sand banks the rabbits sat as quietly as little gray sculptured stones. And then from the direction of the state highway came the sound of footsteps on crisp sycamore leaves. The rabbits hurried noiselessly for cover.

Compare the movement of the rabbits to actions of George and Lennie.

2. "But you ain't gonna get in no trouble, because if you do, I won't let you tend the rabbits." How does George use the rabbits to manipulate Lennie?

3. "O.K—O.K. I'll tell ya again. I ain't got nothing to do. Might jus' as well spen' all my time tellin' you things and then you forget 'em, and I tell you again."

"Tried and tried," said Lennie, "but it didn't do no good. I remember about the rabbits, George."

"The hell with the rabbits. That's all you ever can remember is them rabbits. O.K.! Now you listen and this time you got to remember so we don't get in no trouble. You remember settin' in that gutter on Howard Street and watchin' that blackboard?"

Why is it significant that rabbits are "all [Lennie] can ever remember"? What does this suggest about Lennie?

Of Mice And Men Chapter 1: Elements of Fiction & Literary Devices Page 2

4. "Jus' wanted to feel that girl's dress—jus' wanted to pet it like it was a mouse—Well, how the hell did she know you jus' wanted to feel her dress? She jerks back and you hold on like it was a mouse. She yells and we got to hide in a irrigation ditch all day with guys lookin' for us, and we got to sneak out in the dark and get outa the country. All the time somethin' like that—all the time. I wisht I could put you in a cage with about a million mice an' let you have fun."

The chapter also includes a mention of keeping caged rabbits in a hutch. What is the connection between mice and rabbits? Between the girl's dress and rabbits? Why are they appealing to Lennie?

5. "An' live off the fatta the lan'," Lennie shouted. "An' have rabbits. Go on, George! Tell about what we're gonna have in the garden and about the rabbits in the cages and about the rain in the winter and the stove, and how thick the cream is on the milk like you can hardly cut it. Tell about that, George."

"Why'n't you do it yourself? You know all of it." "No . . . . you tell it. It ain't the same if I tell it. Go on . . . . George. How I get to tend the rabbits."

"Well," said George, "we'll have a big vegetable patch and a rabbit hutch and chickens. And when it rains in the winter, we'll just say the hell with goin' to work, and we'll build up a fire in the stove and set around it an' listen to the rain comin' down on the roof—Nuts!" He took out his pocket knife. "I ain't got time for no more." He drove his knife through the top of one of the bean cans, sawed out the top and passed the can to Lennie. Then he opened a second can. From his side pocket he brought out two spoons and passed one of them to Lennie.

How are the rabbits emblematic of this dream? What does the dream represent to Lennie and George?

6. "Let's have different color rabbits, George."

"Sure we will," George said sleepily. "Red and blue and green rabbits, Lennie. Millions of 'em."

"Furry ones, George, like I seen in the fair in Sacramento." "Sure, furry ones."

What does George's exaggeration about the rabbits suggest about his actual view of the "fatta the lan'" dream?

Of Mice And Men Chapter 1:
Elements of Fiction & Literary Devices Suggested Answers

One of the primary motifs in the novel is rabbits. Consider the following passages and what meaning the references to rabbits creates in the novel.

1. On the sand banks the rabbits sat as quietly as little gray sculptured stones. And then from the direction of the state highway came the sound of footsteps on crisp sycamore leaves. The rabbits hurried noiselessly for cover.

Compare the movement of the rabbits to that of George and Lennie.
George and Lennie have never been able to settle down because they are inevitably chased out of everywhere they try to live. Their lives can be thought of as sitting on one farm or in one town "as quietly as little gray sculptured stones" until Lennie does something that forces them to "hurry noiselessly for cover". The movement of the rabbits is therefore a metaphor for the life that George and Lennie lead.

2. "But you ain't gonna get in no trouble, because if you do, I won't let you tend the rabbits."
How does George use the rabbits to manipulate Lennie?
Lennie's biggest dream in life is to own and take care of rabbits. George knows how important this dream is to Lennie, and therefore is able to manipulate Lennie into doing what he wants by dangling this dream in front of him and then threatening to take it away. It is also somewhat parental—requiring good behavior for a reward.

3. "O.K—O.K. I'll tell ya again. I ain't got nothing to do. Might jus' as well spen' all my time tellin' you things and then you forget 'em, and I tell you again."

"Tried and tried," said Lennie, "but it didn't do no good. I remember about the rabbits, George."

"The hell with the rabbits. That's all you ever can remember is them rabbits. O.K.! Now you listen and this time you got to remember so we don't get in no trouble. You remember settin' in that gutter on Howard Street and watchin' that blackboard?"

Why is it significant that rabbits are "all [Lennie] can ever remember"? What does this suggest about Lennie?
To Lennie, it is not important where he's been or where he's going. Lennie even forgets who his own Aunt is when George has to remind him that it's she who used to give him pet mice. Lennie never forgets about his dream of having rabbits though, to the point where he's memorized George's speech about them. This shows how important this dream of rabbits is to Lennie. He has clearly been described as slow-minded in this chapter, so the fact that "rabbits are all [Lennie] can ever remember" shows his dedication to achieving his rabbit-filled dream.

4. "Jus' wanted to feel that girl's dress—jus' wanted to pet it like it was a mouse—Well, how the hell did she know you jus' wanted to feel her dress? She jerks back and you hold on like it was a mouse. She yells and we got to hide in a irrigation ditch all day with guys lookin' for us, and we got to sneak out in the dark and get outa the country. All the time somethin' like that—all the time. I wisht I could put you in a cage with about a million mice an' let you have fun."

The chapter also includes a mention of keeping caged rabbits in a hutch. What is the connection between mice and rabbits? Between the girl's dress and rabbits? Why are they appealing to Lennie?

Mice and rabbits are two things that bring Lennie comfort – mice because Lennie can pet them and rabbits because Lennie can think about a future of petting and tending to them. Lennie thought of the girl's dress in much the same way, as an object that can comfort him if he pets it. Rabbits, mice, and the girl's dress are all appealing to Lennie because he is comforted by the contact he can have with the soft things.

5. "An' live off the fatta the lan'," Lennie shouted. "An' have rabbits. Go on, George! Tell about what we're gonna have in the garden and about the rabbits in the cages and about the rain in the winter and the stove, and how thick the cream is on the milk like you can hardly cut it. Tell about that, George."

"Why'n't you do it yourself? You know all of it." "No . . . . you tell it. It ain't the same if I tell it. Go on . . . . George. How I get to tend the rabbits."

"Well," said George, "we'll have a big vegetable patch and a rabbit hutch and chickens. And when it rains in the winter, we'll just say the hell with goin' to work, and we'll build up a fire in the stove and set around it an' listen to the rain comin' down on the roof—Nuts!" He took out his pocket knife. "I ain't got time for no more." He drove his knife through the top of one of the bean cans, sawed out the top and passed the can to Lennie. Then he opened a second can. From his side pocket he brought out two spoons and passed one of them to Lennie.

How are the rabbits emblematic of this dream? What does the dream represent to Lennie and George?

To Lennie and George, this dream represents an idyllic life free of unwanted work and responsibility. Rabbits are emblematic of this dream because of their apparent freedom. They are creatures of the land that are not tied down by anything else, and are therefore a metaphor for the life that Lennie and George wish for themselves.

6. "Let's have different color rabbits, George."
"Sure we will," George said sleepily. "Red and blue and green rabbits, Lennie. Millions of 'em."
"Furry ones, George, like I seen in the fair in Sacramento." "Sure, furry ones."
What does George's exaggeration about the rabbits suggest about his actual view of the "fatta the lan'" dream?

George's exaggeration about the rabbits suggests that he does not believe the "fat of the lan'" dream will actually come true. When Lennie brings the dream up, George goes along with whatever Lennie says, but does not discuss the dream in a way that suggests he truly believes it is achievable. In telling Lennie they'll have millions of impossibly colored rabbits, George hints that the dream itself is impossible to achieve.

Of Mice And Men Chapter 1
Reading Activity 7: Meaning and Inferences

Anchor Standard	8th Grade	9th-10th Grade
CCRA.R.1	RL.8.1	RL.9-10.1
CCRA.SL.1	SL.8.1	SL.9-10.1

Objective
Students will answer questions about selected passages from the text which require them to extract meaning or inferences from the text.

Directions
The following pages contain passages from Chapter 1 of Of Mice and Men and questions related to the passages that require close reading to answer. Students should answer the questions related to the passages.

This can be done as a whole-class activity, individually, or in small groups. If it is done individually or in small groups, come together as a class to discuss the answers to the questions.

Follow-Up/Assessment/Extension
Collect the worksheets for review and/or grading.

Of Mice And Men Chapter 1: Meaning & Inferences 1

Read the passages and answer the related questions.

1. *"Then he replaced his hat, pushed himself back from the river, drew up his knees and embraced them. Lennie, who had been watching, imitated George exactly. He pushed himself back, drew up his knees, embraced them, looked over to George to see whether he had it just right. He pulled his hat down a little more over his eyes, the way George's hat was."*

Why does Lennie imitate George's mannerisms multiple times in the chapter? Why is this a regular occurrence for him?

2. *"Lennie looked timidly over to him. "George?"*
"Yeah, what ya want?"
"Where we goin', George?"
The little man jerked down the brim of his hat and scowled over at Lennie. "So you forgot that awready, did you? I gotta tell you again, do I? Jesus Christ, you're a crazy bastard!"
"I forgot," Lennie said softly. "I tried not to forget. Honest to God I did, George."
"O.K—O.K. I'll tell ya again. I ain't got nothing to do. Might jus' as well spen' all my time tellin' you things and then you forget 'em, and I tell you again."
"Tried and tried," said Lennie, "but it didn't do no good. I remember about the rabbits, George."

Why does Lennie forget?

3. *"O.K.," said George. "An' you ain't gonna do no bad things like you done in Weed, neither." Lennie looked puzzled. "Like I done in Weed?" "Oh, so ya forgot that too, did ya? Well, I ain't gonna remind ya, fear ya do it again." A light of understanding broke on Lennie's face. "They run us outa Weed," he exploded triumphantly. "Run us out, hell," said George disgustedly. "We run. They was lookin' for us, but they didn't catch us."*

What happened in Weed? What can a reader infer that Lennie was accused of doing?

4. *George put his hand on Lennie's shoulder. "I ain't takin' it away jus' for meanness. That mouse ain't fresh, Lennie; and besides, you've broke it pettin' it. You get another mouse that's fresh and I'll let you keep it a little while."*

What doesn't Lennie understand about keeping the mouse? Why does he want it, yet a fake mouse is not acceptable to him?

5. *Lennie sat down on the ground and hung his head dejectedly. "I don't know where there is no other mouse. I remember a lady used to give 'em to me—ever' one she got. But that lady ain't here." George scoffed. "Lady, huh? Don't even remember who that lady was. That was your own Aunt Clara. An' she stopped givin' 'em to ya. You always killed 'em."*

Who is Aunt Clara? Where is she?

Of Mice And Men Chapter 1: Meaning & Inferences 1 Suggested Answers

Read the passages and answer the related questions.

1. *"Then he replaced his hat, pushed himself back from the river, drew up his knees and embraced them. Lennie, who had been watching, imitated George exactly. He pushed himself back, drew up his knees, embraced them, looked over to George to see whether he had it just right. He pulled his hat down a little more over his eyes, the way George's hat was."*

Why does Lennie imitate George's mannerisms multiple times in the chapter? Why is this a regular occurrence for him?
Lennie imitates George because he looks to him as a leader and a role model. George is Lennie's closest (and only) companion, and because of this he may feel that he has to impress George and act in a way that is agreeable to him. The need for George's approval is seen in the remorse Lennie displays when George yells at him for asking for ketchup, and is further proof that Lennie imitates George's mannerisms in order to gain approval from his role model.

2. *"Lennie looked timidly over to him. "George?"*
"Yeah, what ya want?"
"Where we goin', George?"
The little man jerked down the brim of his hat and scowled over at Lennie. "So you forgot that awready, did you? I gotta tell you again, do I? Jesus Christ, you're a crazy bastard!"
"I forgot," Lennie said softly. "I tried not to forget. Honest to God I did, George."
"O.K—O.K. I'll tell ya again. I ain't got nothing to do. Might jus' as well spen' all my time tellin' you things and then you forget 'em, and I tell you again."
"Tried and tried," said Lennie, "but it didn't do no good. I remember about the rabbits, George."

Why does Lennie forget?
Lennie forgets where he and George are going because their location and travel is not important to him. From this first chapter, it is clear that Lennie can only remember the things that mean something to him, which is why he remembers his dream of having a farm with rabbits so well. However, George and Lennie's entire lives are spent traveling around the country and doing the same type of physical labor, so their current location does not matter to Lennie because all the farms are the same to him. Though Lennie may not have intellect, he has strong feelings, and he recalls joyful comforts.

3. *"O.K.," said George. "An' you ain't gonna do no bad things like you done in Weed, neither." Lennie looked puzzled. "Like I done in Weed?" "Oh, so ya forgot that too, did ya? Well, I ain't gonna remind ya, fear ya do it again." A light of understanding broke on Lennie's face. "They run us outa Weed," he exploded triumphantly. "Run us out, hell," said George disgustedly. "We run. They was lookin' for us, but they didn't catch us."*

What happened in Weed? What can a reader infer that Lennie was accused of doing?
Lennie grabbed the hem of a woman's dress because it was soft and he wanted to pet it. This action caused Lennie and George to be chased out of town, which allows the reader to infer that the woman misinterpreted Lennie's actions as attempted rape.

Of Mice And Men Chapter 1: Meaning & Inferences 1 Suggested Answers Page 2

4. *George put his hand on Lennie's shoulder. "I ain't takin' it away jus' for meanness. That mouse ain't fresh, Lennie; and besides, you've broke it pettin' it. You get another mouse that's fresh and I'll let you keep it a little while."*

What doesn't Lennie understand about keeping the mouse? Why does he want it, yet a fake mouse is not acceptable to him?
Lennie does not understand the reason that it is bad for him to keep the mouse. For him, the dead mouse is merely a soft thing to pet and comfort him; he does not realize or care that the mouse is broken and old. A fake mouse is not acceptable to Lennie because he only likes to pet things that are soft. A fake mouse would not bring Lennie comfort because it isn't soft like a real mouse is. It also technically would not be a pet or a companion. It would be inanimate and less personal—something that he would not have a relationship with.

5. *Lennie sat down on the ground and hung his head dejectedly. "I don't know where there is no other mouse. I remember a lady used to give 'em to me—ever' one she got. But that lady ain't here." George scoffed. "Lady, huh? Don't even remember who that lady was. That was your own Aunt Clara. An' she stopped givin' 'em to ya. You always killed 'em."*

Who is Aunt Clara? Where is she?
Aunt Clara is Lennie's aunt, whom he does not remember. When Lennie was younger she used to give him pet mice to play with, but he always killed them. The reader would assume that she is either dead or still living where Lennie grew up.

Of Mice And Men Chapter 1: Meaning & Inferences 2

Read the passage and answer the related questions.

A few miles south of Soledad, the Salinas River drops in close to the hillside bank and runs deep and green. The water is warm too, for it has slipped twinkling over the yellow sands in the sunlight before reaching the narrow pool. On one side of the river the golden foothill slopes curve up to the strong and rocky Gabilan Mountains, but on the valley side the water is lined with trees— willows fresh and green with every spring, carrying in their lower leaf junctures the debris of the winter's flooding; and sycamores with mottled, white, recumbent limbs and branches that arch over the pool. On the sandy bank under the trees the leaves lie deep and so crisp that a lizard makes a great skittering if he runs among them. Rabbits come out of the brush to sit on the sand in the evening, and the damp flats are covered with the night tracks of 'coons, and with the spreadpads of dogs from the ranches, and with the split-wedge tracks of deer that come to drink in the dark.

There is a path through the willows and among the sycamores, a path beaten hard by boys coming down from the ranches to swim in the deep pool, and beaten hard by tramps who come wearily down from the highway in the evening to jungle-up near water. In front of the low horizontal limb of a giant sycamore there is an ash pile made by many fires; the limb is worn smooth by men who have sat on it.

Evening of a hot day started the little wind to moving among the leaves. The shade climbed up the hills toward the top. On the sand banks the rabbits sat as quietly as little gray sculptured stones. And then from the direction of the state highway came the sound of footsteps on crisp sycamore leaves. The rabbits hurried noiselessly for cover. A stilted heron labored up into the air and pounded down river. For a moment the place was lifeless, and then two men emerged from the path and came into the opening by the green pool.

1. Is the landscape Steinbeck describes pastoral? Is it hospitable or inhospitable?

2. What evidence is there of human encroachment on nature? Why is it significant?

3. Enumerate mentions of cyclical occurrences in the passage. What are these references suggesting about time?

Of Mice And Men Chapter 1: Meaning & Inferences 2 Suggested Answers

A few miles south of Soledad, the Salinas River drops in close to the hillside bank and runs deep and green. The water is warm too, for it has slipped twinkling over the yellow sands in the sunlight before reaching the narrow pool. On one side of the river the golden foothill slopes curve up to the strong and rocky Gabilan Mountains, but on the valley side the water is lined with trees— willows fresh and green with every spring, carrying in their lower leaf junctures the debris of the winter's flooding; and sycamores with mottled, white, recumbent limbs and branches that arch over the pool. On the sandy bank under the trees the leaves lie deep and so crisp that a lizard makes a great skittering if he runs among them. Rabbits come out of the brush to sit on the sand in the evening, and the damp flats are covered with the night tracks of 'coons, and with the spreadpads of dogs from the ranches, and with the split-wedge tracks of deer that come to drink in the dark.

There is a path through the willows and among the sycamores, a path beaten hard by boys coming down from the ranches to swim in the deep pool, and beaten hard by tramps who come wearily down from the highway in the evening to jungle-up near water. In front of the low horizontal limb of a giant sycamore there is an ash pile made by many fires; the limb is worn smooth by men who have sat on it.

Evening of a hot day started the little wind to moving among the leaves. The shade climbed up the hills toward the top. On the sand banks the rabbits sat as quietly as little gray sculptured stones. And then from the direction of the state highway came the sound of footsteps on crisp sycamore leaves. The rabbits hurried noiselessly for cover. A stilted heron labored up into the air and pounded down river. For a moment the place was lifeless, and then two men emerged from the path and came into the opening by the green pool.

1. Is the landscape Steinbeck describes pastoral? Is it hospitable or inhospitable?
The landscape that Steinbeck describes does seem to be pastoral, as it presents a beautiful, serene, and ideal view of the countryside. This landscape is also very much hospitable. It is teeming with plants and wildlife, and it has supported many people who have come through such as the boys from the ranches and the tramps from the highway. It is presented like a Garden of Eden.

2. What evidence is there of human encroachment on nature? Why is it significant?
The pieces of evidence of human encroachment on nature are the path beaten by the people who have come to be the pool, and the limb of the sycamore worn smooth by men who have sat on it. This is significant because the path and worn limb are the only two blemishes on an otherwise flawless landscape, and they are created by people, specifically people who are displaced and without a permanent home, transients, migrant workers, and hobos.

3. Enumerate mentions of cyclical occurrences in the passage. What are these references suggesting about time?
The debris from winter's flooding, the leaves that have dropped from previous autumns, and the shade creeping over the landscape are three cyclical occurrences that are mentioned in the passage. These references suggest that despite everything that occurs in the lives of people who may pass through this picturesque location, the landscape will continue the way it always has. The leaves will fall from the sycamore trees, the river will flood and debris will wash upon the shore, and the landscape will continue to be an oasis despite whatever may happen to the people who pass through.

Of Mice And Men Chapter 1
Writing Activity 1: What is Friendship?

Anchor Standard	8th Grade	9th-10th Grade
CCRA.SL.1	SL.8.1, 1a-1d	SL.9-10.1, 1a-1d
CCRA.SL.3	SL.8.4	SL.9-10.4
CCRA.W.1	W.8.2	W.9-10.2
CCRA.W.2	W.8.4	W.9-10.4
CCRA.W.4	W.8.5	W.9-10.5
CCRA.W.5		W.9-10.7
		W.9-10.9, 9b

Objectives
- Students will evaluate and analyze textual evidence to define the concept of friendship within the parameters of the novel.
- Students will evaluate passages that reveal characterization, motive and conflict.
- Students will examine language for ways in which characterization, motive and conflict illuminate the main theme of friendship in the novel.
- Students will write a composition in which they consider their analysis of relevant passages to answer the question, "What is friendship?"

Directions
The following series of worksheets and information organizers can be used by students individually, in small groups, or done partly as a whole-class activity. They are intended to guide students through the process of reading and thinking critically about information by ultimately answering the single question, "What is friendship?"

Preview the following pages. Determine the best way to have your particular class handle this assignment (individually, pairs, groups, whole-class, or some combination). A combination of group work (to do the analyzing of the text on the chart page) followed by individual work (to do the second and third pages of the assignment) would most likely be best to fulfill the standards listed for this assignment.

Follow-Up/Assessment/Extension
- The written assignment will be a good basis for assessment of the students' success with this assignment. Create a rubric explaining the criteria on which their written assignments will be evaluated.
- Tell students to continue observing examples of when characters demonstrate friendship to one another, especially as more characters are introduced.
- Have some students read/present their writing assignments to the class to practice more speaking/listening skills and to expose all students to each others' ideas.
- Use this assignment to introduce the idea of the responsibilities that being part of a friendship entails.

Of Mice And Men Chapter 1: What Is Friendship?

Chapter 1 introduces traveling companions and friends George and Lennie. Their interaction shows that they are interdependent on one another in different ways. Their friendship, however, is not without conflicts. Through characterization, motive and conflict, a larger theme of friendship emerges in the novel. Close reading of detail can uncover layers of meaning important to understanding a novel's themes. This writing assignment will explore the nature of friendship as depicted in the novel.

Using textual evidence from chapter 1, look for important but perhaps seemingly insignificant details to answer to the question "What is friendship?"

To explore the concept of friendship:

1. Identify passages and quotes which offer details about or insights into the characters' friendship. Look particularly for moments of conflict.

2. Examine the context of your quotes.

3. Consider the connotation and denotation of key phrases in your quotes.

   a. Is there conflict? How does it get resolved?
   b. Does the language suggest that the characters are equals or not equals?
   c. How do characters address one another?
   d. What qualities of friendship (loyalty, honesty) are present in the passage?
   e. Is their friendship threatened? If so, by what?

Of Mice And Men Chapter 1: What Is Friendship?

Use Your Own Knowledge

1. What does friendship mean to you?

2. What are the qualities of a good friend?

3. What are the responsibilities of a good friend?

Review the chapter and compare George and Lennie on the criteria in the middle column. List examples from the text to back up your claims.

George	Point of Comparison	Lennie
	Is he kind?	
	Is he helpful?	
	Is he loyal?	
	Is he truthful?	

Of Mice And Men Chapter 1: What Is Friendship?

Complete as many of these charts as you need to analyze all the information about friendship between George and Lennie. Find quotes from the text where conflict occurs between the characters.

Quote (and page number)	Paraphrase Quote	What is revealed about the speaker of the quote?	How does the speaker's attitude affect their friendship?

Of Mice And Men Chapter 1
Suggested Writing Assignments

Anchor Standard	8th Grade	9th-10th Grade
CCRA.W.1	W.8.1, 1a-1d	W.9-10.1, 1a-1e
CCRA W.2	W.8.2, 2a-2f	W.9-10.2, 2a-2f
CCRA.W.3	W.8.3, 3a-3e	W.9-10.3, 3a-3e
CCRA.W.4	W.8.4	W.9-10.4
CCRA.W.5	W.8.5	W.9-10.5

Objective
Students will be assigned or will choose one of a selection of writing assignments pertaining to Chapter 1 of *Of Mice and Men* to fulfill one or more of the standards listed above.

Directions
To provide you with maximum flexibility for differentiated instruction, the following page has a list of suggested writing assignments, all related to Chapter 1 of *Of Mice and Men*. Either assign individual students particular assignments to do or allow students to choose their own assignments.

A second page of "Quick Write" topics is also included.

Follow-Up/Assessment/Extension
- Have dramatic readings of students' narratives or poems.
- Create a "reading room" space in your classroom where students can donate their writing assignments for others in the class to read.
- Allow students to do more than one assignment if they want to.
- Use the "left-over" assignments (not chosen for this activity) as topics for journal entries.

Of Mice And Men Chapter 1: Creative Analytical Writing Assignments

1. Write a flashback scene about the time that Aunt Clara gave Lennie a rubber mouse.

2. Write a scene in dialogue of a conversation between Lennie and George as they are being pursued as they flee Weed.

3. Write a paragraph that explains how George became a traveling laborer.

4. What is George's real dream, finding a nice girl? Describe it in a paragraph.

5. Define what responsibilities are inherent in friendship.

6. Imagine that you are Lennie. Describe the way you see the world.

7. Describe the relationship between George and Lennie.

8. Write a paragraph that speculates why George feels so much anger.

9. Write a campfire story that George might tell Lennie.

10. George and Lennie are essentially homeless migrant workers. Write a paragraph about ways in which they might struggle.

Of Mice And Men Chapter 1: Quick-Write Writing Assignments

1. Why is the natural setting of the landscape emphasized?

2. What is the relationship between man and nature in this chapter?

3. Is George's frustration with Lennie justified? Why?

4. What does it mean to live off "the fatta the lan'"?

5. Why is their dream to have a permanent home? What does this suggest about their lives as migrant workers?

6. Contrast the two men physically. Why is the contrast significant?

7. How are the men compared to animals? Why is the comparison significant?

8. Consider George asking Lennie to remember their camping location as a future hiding place. What do you suspect might happen?

9. Comment on Lennie's dishonesty.

10. Comment on Lennie's remorse and willingness to live in a cave.

NOTES
OF MICE AND MEN

MATERIALS: CHAPTER 2
OF MICE AND MEN

Reading Activity 1: True or False?

Reading Activity 2: Analyzing Passages

Reading Activity 3: Physical Attributes & Characterization

Reading Activity 4: Action, Character, Decision

Reading Activity 5: Figurative Language

Reading Activity 6: Elements of Fiction & Literary Devices

Reading Activity 7: Meaning and Inferences

Writing Activity 1: What Is Masculinity?

Suggested Writing Assignments

Quick-Write Assignments

NOTES
OF MICE AND MEN

Of Mice And Men Chapter 2
Reading Activity 1: True or False?

Anchor Standard	8th Grade	9th-10th Grade
CCRA.R.1	RL.8.1	RL.9-10.1
CCRA.SL.1	SL.8.1	SL.9-10.1
CCRA.SL.4	SL.8.4	SL.9-10.4

Objectives
- Students will be able to cite the parts of the text that support their analysis of what the text says or infers.
- Students will consider statements about the text, determine whether those statements are true or false, and will give textual evidence supporting their choices.
- Students will work together in small groups to discuss, analyze, and evaluate the statements made.
- Students will evaluate the analytical work of their peers.

Directions
Prior to reading Chapter 2: Give students (or post) the following list of statements about the chapters, and explain to students that they should read Chapter 2 to find out if these statements are true or false:

> George and Lennie are cousins.
> Candy has a little puppy.
> Candy is a gossip.
> George is a gossip.
> Curley's wife is quiet and modest.
> Slim killed some puppies.

After reading Chapter 2: The worksheets on the following pages can be done by students individually, in small groups, or as a whole class. Below are directions to use the questions as a group activity to fulfill more state standards:

- Cut the worksheet apart, making each question and answer box a slip.
- Divide your class into six groups and give one question and a True/False evaluation form to each group. Tell students they are to discuss the statement and determine if the statement is true or false, supporting their decision with evidence from the text. Tell them their answers will be evaluated on the criteria given on the evaluation form.
- Give students ample time to discuss the statements and record their answers.
- Have the groups swap True or False question slips so that each group can evaluate another group's answer. The group should fill in the number of the question they are evaluating, decide how well the answer fulfills the criteria listed, and fill out the form accordingly.
- Repeat the previous step until all the groups have evaluated each others' answers.
- Collect the evaluations and answer slips.

Of Mice And Men Chapter 2: True or False?

Write *True* or *False* in the blank next to each statement. Below the statement, explain why you chose true or false, referencing the text to support your choices.

_____ 1. George and Lennie are cousins.

_____ 2. Candy has a little puppy.

_____ 3. Candy is a gossip.

Of Mice And Men Chapter 2 True or False? Page 2

_____ 4. George is a gossip.

_____ 5. Curley's wife is quiet and modest.

_____ 6. Slim killed some puppies.

Of Mice And Men Chapter 2 True or False? Evaluation

List Your Group's Members: Your Group's Question # _____

_____   _____   _____

_____   _____   _____

1 = No, Not At All **2** = A Little **3** = Some **4** = Yes **5** = Yes, Very Well

Evaluation of Question # ___
Does the explanation support the answer of true or false?   1 2 3 4 5
Is there good textual evidence to support the answer?   1 2 3 4 5
Is the answer clearly stated?   1 2 3 4 5
                                Total Score _____ of a possible 15 points

Evaluation of Question # ___
Does the explanation support the answer of true or false?   1 2 3 4 5
Is there good textual evidence to support the answer?   1 2 3 4 5
Is the answer clearly stated?   1 2 3 4 5
                                Total Score _____ of a possible 15 points

Evaluation of Question # ___
Does the explanation support the answer of true or false?   1 2 3 4 5
Is there good textual evidence to support the answer?   1 2 3 4 5
Is the answer clearly stated?   1 2 3 4 5
                                Total Score _____ of a possible 15 points

Evaluation of Question # ___
Does the explanation support the answer of true or false?   1 2 3 4 5
Is there good textual evidence to support the answer?   1 2 3 4 5
Is the answer clearly stated?   1 2 3 4 5
                                Total Score _____ of a possible 15 points

Evaluation of Question # ___
Does the explanation support the answer of true or false?   1 2 3 4 5
Is there good textual evidence to support the answer?   1 2 3 4 5
Is the answer clearly stated?   1 2 3 4 5
                                Total Score _____ of a possible 15 points

Of Mice And Men Chapter 2: True or False? Suggested Answers

Write *True* or *False* in the blank next to each statement. Below the statement, explain why you chose true or false, referencing the text to support your choices.

FALSE 1. George and Lennie are cousins.

> This is false; George and Lennie are not cousins. When the ranch boss asks why George takes so much interest in Lennie, George says they're cousins as an excuse, but when Lennie later asks George if that was true, George says "that was a lie. An' I'm damn glad it was. If I was a relative of yours I'd shoot myself."

FALSE 2. Candy has a little puppy.

> Candy does not have a little puppy, but rather "a hell of an old dog," according to George. The dog is blind, has trouble walking, and has an old moth-eaten coat. Further, Candy says "he was a good sheep dog when he was younger."

TRUE 3. Candy is a gossip.

> Candy is most definitely a gossip, as is seen when he tells George and Lennie all about Curley, the boss' son, and his willingness to fight. When Candy tells George "Don't tell Curley I said none of this. He'd slough me," it is clear that Candy often gossips about people.

TRUE 4. George is a gossip.

> George is also a gossip, as is seen in his engagement with the gossip Candy is telling. When Candy brings up the nature of Curley's wife, George says: "'You won't tell Curley nothing I said? […] Well, you look her over, mister. You see if she ain't a tart'". George's interest in Candy's gossip and his willingness to jump in with some gossip of his own shows that he enjoys talking about other people behind their back.

Of Mice And Men Chapter 2 True or False? Suggested Answers Page 2

<u>FALSE</u> 5. Curley's wife is quiet and modest.

Curley's wife is flirtatious, open, and is not afraid to expose herself. When Candy talks to George about her, he says that she gives "the eye" to men all around the ranch. After George has met her, he remarks: "I seen 'em poison before, but I never seen no piece of jail bait worse than her." Even after the brief encounter the reader has had with her, it is clear that Curley's wife is anything but quiet and modest.

<u>TRUE</u> 6. Slim killed some puppies.

This is true. Slim has a dog, Lulu, that just gave birth to nine pups. According to Slim, he "drowned four of 'em right off. She couldn't feed that many."

Of Mice And Men Chapter 2
Reading Activity 2: Analyzing Passages

Anchor Standard	8th Grade	9th-10th Grade
CCRA.R.6	RL.8.1	RL.9-10.1
	RL.8.3	
	RL.8.4	RL.9-10.4
	RL.8.6	
CCRA.SL.1	SL.8.1	SL.9-10.1

Objectives
- Students will analyze what the text says explicitly as well as inferences drawn from the text.
- Students will analyze how different points of view of the characters and the audience (or reader) creates suspense or humor.
- Students will analyze the impact of specific word choices on meaning and tone.

Directions
On the pages that follow, there are 8 passages to analyze, each with a question or questions to guide the process. There are many ways to use these questions:
- You could use them as a worksheet for all students to complete individually.
- You could use the worksheet as your guide in a whole-class discussion. Have students turn to the first passage in the book, read it, then ask the question(s) orally. Repeat through all 8 questions.
- You could assign one passage to each of 8 different groups of students, for the students to discuss and come up with responses to the question(s). Then hold a whole-class discussion.
- You could read the passage and then see which student can find the passage first (to practice skimming skills). Then follow up with the questions(s) and discussion.
- You could have students choose one or two questions to respond to in writing in their notebooks or journals.

Follow-Up/Assessment/Extension
- Have students write about the immediate conflict that Curley created. What is his motive?
- Have students pick out other passages in this chapter that show interesting word usage, descriptions, or lack of clarity.
- As an introduction to this activity and this chapter, ask students to write about how strangers behave when they occupy a space together—a store, an elevator, etc. How do people relate to one another in those contexts?

Of Mice And Men Chapter 2 Analyzing Passages

Answer the questions following the quotations completely.

1. "We travel together," said George coldly.
"Oh, so it's that way."
George was tense and motionless. "Yea, it's that way."

What is Curley inferring? What does Curley not quite understand?

2. "And these shelves were loaded with little articles, soap and talcum powder, razors and those Western magazines ranch men love to read and scoff at and secretly believe."

What does the contradiction about the magazines suggest about men like George?

3. "I wasn't kicked in the head with no horse, was I, George?"
"Be a damn good thing if you was," George said viciously. "Save ever'body a hell of a lot of trouble."

What are the connotations of the word "vicious," and how do they shape the reader's view of George?

4. "Well, that glove's fulla Vaseline."
"Vaseline? What the hell for?"
"Well, I will tell ya what—Curley says he's keepin' that hand soft for his wife."

What are Candy and George's reactions to this supposed fact about Curley? How does it shape their perception of him?

Of Mice And Men Chapter 2 Analyzing Passages Page 2

5. "The swamper considered… "Well . . . tell you what. Curley's like a lot of little guys. He hates big guys. He's alla time picking scraps with big guys. Kind of like he's mad at 'em because he ain't a big guy. You seen little guys like that, ain't you? Always scrappy?"

According to Candy's logic, what does "scrappy" mean? What motivates Curley to behave this way, in Candy's estimation?

_____
_____
_____

6. "…he moved with a majesty only achieved by royalty and master craftsman. He was a jerkline skinner, the prince of the ranch, capable of driving ten, sixteen, even twenty mules with a single line to the leaders. He was capable of killing a fly on the wheeler's butt with a bull whip without touching the mule. There was a gravity in his manner and a quiet so profound that all talk stopped when he spoke, His authority was so great that his word was taken on any subject, be it politics or love. This was Slim, the jerkline skinner."

What is the tone of this passage? What does it suggest about masculinity?

_____
_____
_____

7. "She slang her pups last night," said Slim. "Nine of 'em. I drowned four of 'em right off. She couldn't feed that many." Is this more shocking or compassionate?

What does the action of drowning the puppies suggest about Slim?

_____
_____
_____

8. "Lennie's eyes moved down over her body, and though she didn't seem to be looking at Lennie she bridled a little. She looked at her fingers. "Sometimes Curley's in here," she explained. George said brusquely, "Well he ain't now."

"If he ain't, I guess I better look someplace else," she said playfully.

Lennie watched her, fascinated. George said, "If I see him, I'll pass the word you was looking for him."

She smiled archly and twitched her body. "Nobody can't blame a person for lookin'," she said. There were footsteps behind her, going by. She turned her head. "Hi, Slim," she said."

What does Curley's wife's retort ("nobody can't…") suggest about her views on marital fidelity?

Of Mice And Men Chapter 2 Analyzing Passages

Answer the questions following the quotations completely.

1. "We travel together," said George coldly.
"Oh, so it's that way."
George was tense and motionless. "Yea, it's that way."

What is Curley inferring? What does Curley not quite understand?
Curley is inferring that George and Lennie's relationship is somehow different or wrong, but they rely on each other and depend on one another. What Curley does not quite understand is the love and care that the two have for each other. He says their dependence on each other as a sign of weakness, but does not see the benefits of having someone who cares about you.

2. "And these shelves were loaded with little articles, soap and talcum powder, razors and those Western magazines ranch men love to read and scoff at and secretly believe." What does the contradiction about the magazines suggest about men like George?
This contradiction suggests that men like George think of other people's opinions of them as being of the utmost importance. If they believe what they read in a magazine, but have to pretend they don't actually buy what it says, then it is clear that they place more importance on everyone else's opinion of them than they do on being honest with people.

3. "I wasn't kicked in the head with no horse, was I, George?"

"Be a damn good thing if you was," George said viciously. "Save ever'body a hell of a lot of trouble."

What are the connotations of the word "vicious," and how do they shape the reader's view of George?
In this case, the connotation of the word "vicious" seems to be "said with the intent to be hurtful." George's words to Lennie said in this vicious manner show that George is not always caring and compassionate towards Lennie, but can sometimes be violent and hurtful towards him. It also foreshadows that the natural world can be dangerous (i.e. getting kicked by a horse).

4. "Well, that glove's fulla Vaseline."
"Vaseline? What the hell for?"
"Well, I will tell ya what—Curley says he's keepin' that hand soft for his wife."

What are Candy and George's reactions to this supposed fact about Curley? How does it shape their perception of him?
Candy and George are both disgusted by the supposed fact about Curley's Vaseline-filled glove. This shapes their perception of him by making him out to be vulgar, which is how they think of him. They do not see his sexual vulgarity as a positive sign of his masculinity, actually quite the opposite.

5. "The swamper considered... "Well . . . tell you what. Curley's like a lot of little guys. He hates big guys. He's alla time picking scraps with big guys. Kind of like he's mad at 'em because he ain't a big guy. You seen little guys like that, ain't you? Always scrappy?"

According to Candy's logic, what does "scrappy" mean? What motivates Curley to behave this way, in Candy's estimation?
According to Candy, "scrappy" means a little guy who likes to pick fights with people to prove that his size doesn't make him weak. According to Candy, Curley's small size is the driving force behind his aggressive behavior. He is small, so he picks on larger people to prove that just because he is smaller, that doesn't mean he can't take them. Curley seems to feel the need to justify his big ego by being "scrappy" and picking fights with big guys. Curley's "hate" toward larger men is a reflection of his own unhappiness with his small stature.

6. "...he moved with a majesty only achieved by royalty and master craftsman. He was a jerkline skinner, the prince of the ranch, capable of driving ten, sixteen, even twenty mules with a single line to the leaders. He was capable of killing a fly on the wheeler's butt with a bull whip without touching the mule. There was a gravity in his manner and a quiet so profound that all talk stopped when he spoke, His authority was so great that his word was taken on any subject, be it politics or love. This was Slim, the jerkline skinner."

What is the tone of this passage? What does it suggest about masculinity?
The tone of this passage is admiring and almost marveling. Slim is described as the epitome of a masculine, confident, and strong rancher. The tone that this passage takes in describing him gives the reader insight into how other ranchers view him, which is an attitude of reverence in the knowledge of his superiority. Words like "gravity" and "profound" suggest that Slim is an authority figure, and one of God-like stature in the eyes of the ranch hands.

7. "She slang her pups last night," said Slim. "Nine of 'em. I drowned four of 'em right off. She couldn't feed that many."

Is this more shocking or compassionate? What does the action of drowning the puppies suggest about Slim?
At first glimpse, Slim's drowning of the four puppies does come off as rather shocking. He bluntly confesses his murders without seeming to show any remorse or sorrow for what he did. However, when Slim explains that he "drowned four of 'em right off" because the mother would not have been able to support all of the puppies if they had all been kept alive, it becomes clear that Slim's actions are compassionate because the puppies would not have all been able to survive anyway, and they would most likely have had a much more painful death. This action suggests that while Slim is quite hard and tough on the outside, he is truthfully compassionate and caring. This also shows that nature is not always able to provide and care for its creatures.

Of Mice And Men Chapter 2 Analyzing Passages Page 3

8. "Lennie's eyes moved down over her body, and though she didn't seem to be looking at Lennie she bridled a little. She looked at her fingers. "Sometimes Curley's in here," she explained. George said brusquely, "Well he ain't now."

"If he ain't, I guess I better look someplace else," she said playfully.

Lennie watched her, fascinated. George said, "If I see him, I'll pass the word you was looking for him."

She smiled archly and twitched her body. "Nobody can't blame a person for lookin'," she said. There were footsteps behind her, going by. She turned her head. "Hi, Slim," she said."

What does Curley's wife's retort ("nobody can't…") suggest about her views on marital fidelity?
Curley's wife's retort that "nobody can't blame a person for lookin'" clearly has a double meaning. While this retort was meant as a response to her looking for her husband, it can also be applied to Lennie's obvious checking out of the wife. Her reaction to Lennie's actions in this way suggests that she does not place a huge amount of importance on marital fidelity. While she notices it, she is not very put off by Lennie's ogling over her body which leads the reader to assume that she is not easily put off.

Of Mice And Men Chapter 2
Reading Activity 3: Physical Attributes and Characterization

Anchor Standard	8th Grade	9th-10th Grade
CCRA.R.1	RL.8.1	RL.9-10.1
CCRA.SL.1	SL.8.1	SL.9-10.1

Objective
Using textual evidence, students will explore how physical attributes create meaningful characterization.

Directions
The Physical Attributes and Characterization worksheet on the following page could be used in many ways, completed by small groups of students, individual students, or as a whole class activity.

Students will be able to identify how details describing the physical attributes of characters inform their characterization. Students will observe the way Steinbeck presents details about characters' physical attributes, including body, mannerisms, gestures, and clothing. Students can revisit this assignment later in the unit to further investigate how the physical descriptions foreshadow plot events in the novel.

Students will concentrate on 3 of 5 listed characters. This allows students to develop expertise in characters of greatest interest to them, or for teachers to assign specific characters to students for more meaningful investigation. Students may (and should) use their books to skim through the chapter to refresh their memories or gather more information about the characters.

After students complete the worksheets discuss students' answers as a whole class. Collect the worksheets for grading, if you choose, or have students put them in their notebooks for further study.

Follow-Up/Assessment/Extension
Revisit this assignment later in the unit and discuss the relationship between characters' physical descriptions and their morality. Is there a correlation? What is it?

Of Mice And Men Chapter 2
Reading Activity 3: Physical Attributes and Characterization

From the list of characters below, select three. Locate details about these characters' physical appearance in chapter 2. Complete the chart below using this evidence from the text. Then, after reviewing the quotes you selected, write about how these physical attributes form a clearer characterization. Use your books to locate significant details about each character's physical appearance (body, mannerisms, gestures, clothing, etc.).

Candy | Curley | Crooks | Slim | Curley' Wife

Character	Quote 1	Quote 2	Quote 3	How do quotes inform characterization?

Of Mice And Men Chapter 2
Reading Activity 3: Physical Attributes and Characterization
Suggested Answers

From the list of characters below, select three. Locate details about these characters' physical appearance in chapter 2. Complete the chart below using this evidence from the text. Then, after reviewing the quotes you selected, write about how these physical attributes form a clearer characterization. Use your books to locate significant details about each character's physical appearance (body, mannerisms, gestures, clothing, etc.).

Candy | Curley | Crooks | Slim | Curley' Wife

Character	Quote 1	Quote 2	Quote 3	How do quotes inform characterization?
Candy	Many different selections could be made	Many different selections could be made	Many different selections could be made	Quotes about Candy's physical features define him as a frail, older man. This description helps the reader to understand Candy's demeanor as one that an old man who's worked on a ranch his whole life would have—fearful, dependent, yet friendly.
Curley	Many different selections could be made	Many different selections could be made	Many different selections could be made	Quotes about Curley's physical features define him as small and "scrappy", which helps the reader to understand why his small size makes him want to pick on bigger guys. He is insecure about his masculinity.

Crooks	Many different selections could be made	Many different selections could be made	Many different selections could be made	He is explored in greater detail in Chapter 4. He is in chronic pain due to the deformity of his spine. He is black, and this sets him apart from the other men.
Slim	Many different selections could be made	Many different selections could be made	Many different selections could be made	Slim is described as a strong, confident, and all around superior rancher. This description helps the reader characterize him as a leader on the ranch. He is masculinity incarnate—strong but gentle, moral, and kind.
Curley's Wife	Many different selections could be made	Many different selections could be made	Many different selections could be made	Curley's wife's physical features and dress are described as loose and seductive. This helps the reader characterize her as being an object of beauty or desire to be looked at.

Of Mice And Men Chapter 2
Reading Activity 4: Action, Character, Decision

Anchor Standard	8th Grade	9th-10th Grade
CCRA.R.1	RL.8.3	
CCRA.SL.1	SL.8.1	SL.9-10.1

Objective
Students will identify whether particular lines of dialogue or incidents in the story propel the action, reveal aspects of a character, or provoke a decision.

Directions
The following page contains passages from Chapter 2 of Of Mice and Men. Students should determine whether the passages advance the action, reveal aspects of a character, or provoke a decision.

This can be done as a whole-class activity, individually, or in small groups.

Follow-Up/Assessment/Extension
Have students skim Chapter 2 to find one example of a passage that propels the action, one that reveals aspects of a character, and one that provokes a decision. Again, this could be done individually or as a group.

Of Mice And Men Chapter 2: Action, Character, Decision

Write **A** (for Action) **C** (for Character) or **D** (for Decision) in the blank next to each to identify whether the passage/statement advances the action, tells us more about a character, or provokes a decision. On the lines under each question, provide a short explanation of your choice.

____ 1. But don't you try to put nothing over, Milton. I got my eye on you.

____ 2. Don't make no mistake about that. He's the boss's son. Look, Lennie. You try to keep away from him, will you? Don't never speak to him. If he comes in here you move clear to the other side of the room. Will you do that, Lennie?"

____ 3. Carlson stepped back to let Slim precede him, and then the two of them went out the door.

____ 4. "Sure," said George. "I seen plenty tough little guys. But this Curley better not make no mistakes about Lennie. Lennie ain't handy, but this Curley punk is gonna get hurt if he messes around with Lennie."

____ 5. She wore a cotton house dress and red mules, on the insteps of which were little bouquets of red ostrich feathers.

Of Mice And Men Chapter 2:
Action, Character, Decision Suggested Answers

Write **A** (for Action) **C** (for Character) or **D** (for Decision) in the blank next to each to identify whether the passage/statement advances the action, tells us more about a character, or provokes a decision. On the lines under each question, provide a short explanation of your choice.

A 1. But don't you try to put nothing over, Milton. I got my eye on you.
This quote advances the action of the boss threatening George that he'll be watching to make sure George doesn't try to cheat Lennie. In this quote, the boss acts by asserting that he will be keeping tabs on George. This creates conflict between George and the authority figures on the ranch, making George extra self-conscious.

D 2. Don't make no mistake about that. He's the boss's son. Look, Lennie. You try to keep away from him, will you? Don't never speak to him. If he comes in here you move clear to the other side of the room. Will you do that, Lennie?"
In this quote, George decides that Curley is dangerous and because he is liable to pick a fight with Lennie if he gets the chance, Lennie must stay away from him at all costs. Since Lennie lacks the intelligence to get out of a potentially threatening situation, George makes the decision that Curley should be avoided.

C 3. Carlson stepped back to let Slim precede him, and then the two of them went out the door.
This quote provides more information about both Carlson's character and Slim's character. In this quote, Carlson and Slim are leaving the room, but Carlson steps aside to let Slim lead the way. This shows that Slim is a natural leader among the ranchers, and that Carlson accepts that he is a follower.

A 4. "Sure," said George. "I seen plenty tough little guys. But this Curley better not make no mistakes about Lennie. Lennie ain't handy, but this Curley punk is gonna get hurt if he messes around with Lennie."
This quote represents an action because it determines that if Curley and Lennie were to get in a fight, Lennie would absolutely come out on top. While no fight actually takes place within this quote, the action of the fight is advanced because it suggests a conclusion.

C 5. She wore a cotton house dress and red mules, on the insteps of which were little bouquets of red ostrich feathers.
This quote characterizes Curley's wife by describing her outfit. The kind of clothes she wears provides good insight as to what her personality is like, which is flirtatious and open. A dirty barn on a ranch is an inappropriate place to wear such delicate clothing. This suggests that she is out of place. She is also connected to the natural world, through "mules" and "ostrich feathers."

Of Mice And Men Chapter 2
Reading Activity 5: Figurative Language

Anchor Standard	8th Grade	9th-10th Grade
CCRA.R.4	RL.8.4	RL.9-10.4
CCRA.SL.1	SL.8.1	SL.9-10.1

Objectives
- Students will determine the meaning of words and phrases as they are used in the text, including figurative and connotative meanings.
- Students will determine how figurative language contributes to meaning.

Directions
The following page has a passage from the text which includes examples of figurative language. This work-sheet can be done individually, as a whole-class activity, or in small groups. Discuss the answers as a whole class. Collect the worksheets and record the grades if you choose to do so.

Follow-Up/Assessment/Extension
Ask students to begin tracking instances of a particular type of figurative language (personification, metaphor, hyperbole, etc.) in the text. Ask students to make a list to track their observations. Assign students a paper that uses these examples to make an argument about how the language creates meaning.

Of Mice And Men Chapter 2: Figurative Language

Read the following passages and determine if the passage contains a metaphor (M) or simile (S). On the lines below, explain how figurative language creates meaning in the passage.

_____1. At about ten o'clock in the morning the sun threw a bright dust-laden bar through one of the side windows, and in and out of the beam flies shot like rushing stars.

_____2. "No, he ain't, but he's sure a hell of a good worker. Strong as a bull."

_____3. He was a jerkline skinner, the prince of the ranch, capable of driving ten, sixteen, even twenty mules with a single line to the leaders.

_____4. His hands, large and lean, were as delicate in their action as those of a temple dancer.

_____5. The curls, tiny little sausages, were spread on the hay behind her head, and her lips were parted.

Of Mice And Men Chapter 2: Figurative Language Suggested Answers

Read the following passages and determine if the passage contains a metaphor (M) or simile (S). On the lines below, explain how figurative language creates meaning in the passage.

S 1. At about ten o'clock in the morning the sun threw a bright dust-laden bar through one of the side windows, and in and out of the beam flies shot like rushing stars.
This passage contains a simile that compares flies flying around a beam of light to rushing stars. This allows the reader to better picture how the flies are lit up by the beam of light, and to understand this as a beautiful image rather than a dirty or disgusting image as flies could evoke.

S 2. "No, he ain't, but he's sure a hell of a good worker. Strong as a bull."
This passage contains a simile that compares Lennie's strength to the strength of a bull. This simile allows the reader to understand just how strong Lennie is by giving the reader a very recognizable mark of strength.

M 3. He was a jerkline skinner, the prince of the ranch, capable of driving ten, sixteen, even twenty mules with a single line to the leaders.
This passage contains a metaphor because it speaks of Slim as if he were actually a prince. This metaphor serves to make the reader feel the regal and important way in which Slim carries himself, and therefore the way others see him.

S 4. His hands, large and lean, were as delicate in their action as those of a temple dancer.
This passage contains a simile that compares Slim's hands to those of a temple dancer. Comparing Slim to a dancer that uses elegant yet sharp hand motions accents Slim's grace in the rugged farmwork he does. He is a paradox: "large" but "delicate."

M 5. The curls, tiny little sausages, were spread on the hay behind her head, and her lips were parted.
This passage contains a metaphor because it speaks of Curley's wife's curls as if they were actually sausages. Using a metaphor to show that Curley's wife's hair looks so much like sausages helps the reader to form a clearer image of Curley's wife in their head. It is a somewhat vulgar comparison—what woman wants her hair compared to meat; however, a sausage is succulent and meant to be consumed.

Of Mice And Men Chapter 2
Reading Activity 6: Elements of Fiction & Literary Devices

Anchor Standard	8th Grade	9th-10th Grade
CCRA.R.1	RL.8.1	RL.9-10.1
	RL.8.2	RL.9-10.2
	RL.8.3	RL.9-10.4
	RL.8.4	RL.9-10.5
	RL.8.6	
CCRA.SL.1	SL.8.1	SL.9-10.1

Objective
Students will study and discuss passages from the text to examine symbol, motif and theme and explore how these create meaning in the text.

Directions
Use the following discussion questions as a guide to discussing symbol, motif and theme, in these chapters. You can give students the questions ahead of time and have them formulate answers prior to the class discussion or you can jump right in with a whole class discussion without student preparation if your students will handle that well.

As you hold the class discussion, be sure to include conversations defining symbol, motif and theme and explaining how these work together to advance meaning in the text.

Follow-Up/Assessment/Extension
After your discussion, ask students to look for recurrences of these symbols, motifs and themes in future chapters.

Of Mice And Men Chapter 2: Elements of Fiction & Literary Devices

Read the following passages and answer questions, making inferences about the significance of symbols, motifs and themes.

1. "The old man came slowly into the room. He had his broom in his hand. And at his heels there walked a dragfooted sheepdog, gray of muzzle, and with pale, blind old eyes. The dog struggled lamely to the side of the room and lay down, grunting softly to himself and licking his grizzled, moth-eaten coat. The swamper watched him until he was settled. "I wasn't listenin'. I was jus' standin' in the shade a minute scratchin' my dog."

How are Candy and his dog similar? Why is this significant?

_____
_____
_____

2. "Carlson said thoughtfully, "Well, looka here, Slim. I been thinkin'. That dog of Candy's is so God damn old he can't hardly walk. Stinks like hell, too. Ever' time he comes into the bunk house I can smell him for two, three days. Why'n't you get Candy to shoot his old dog and give him one of the pups to raise up? I can smell that dog a mile away. Got no teeth, damn near blind, can't eat. Candy feeds him milk. He can't chew nothing else."

Why does Carlson ask Slim to convince Candy to shoot his dog? How does Carlson justify the act?

_____
_____
_____

3. "After a moment the ancient dog walked lamely in through the open door. He gazed about with mild, half-blind eyes. He sniffed, and then lay down and put his head between his paws. Curley popped into the doorway again and stood looking into the room. The dog raised his head, but when Curley jerked out, the grizzled head sank to the floor again."

a. What does Candy's dog symbolize?

_____
_____
_____

Of Mice And Men Chapter 2: Elements of Fiction & Literary Devices Page 2

b. One of the major conflicts explored in this chapter is man versus the natural world. How is that theme related to Candy's dog?

c. How is the conflict of man versus the natural world related to Slim's dog, Lulu, and her pups?

Of Mice And Men Chapter 2:
Elements of Fiction & Literary Devices Suggested Answers

Read the following passages and answer questions, making inferences about the significance of symbols, motifs and themes.

1. "The old man came slowly into the room. He had his broom in his hand. And at his heels there walked a dragfooted sheepdog, gray of muzzle, and with pale, blind old eyes. The dog struggled lamely to the side of the room and lay down, grunting softly to himself and licking his grizzled, moth-eaten coat. The swamper watched him until he was settled. "I wasn't listenin'. I was jus' standin' in the shade a minute scratchin' my dog."

How are Candy and his dog similar? Why is this significant?
Both Candy and his dog are very old, and don't seem to be of much use around the farm. They also move slowly, and seem to not serve a purpose. This is significant because Candy's similarity to his dog may be the reason for his love and adoration of it. Candy feels empathy with the dog's condition due to his old age, which could account for why he still keeps the dog around despite its decrepit condition.

2. "Carlson said thoughtfully, "Well, looka here, Slim. I been thinkin'. That dog of Candy's is so God damn old he can't hardly walk. Stinks like hell, too. Ever' time he comes into the bunk house I can smell him for two, three days. Why'n't you get Candy to shoot his old dog and give him one of the pups to raise up? I can smell that dog a mile away. Got no teeth, damn near blind, can't eat. Candy feeds him milk. He can't chew nothing else."

Why does Carlson ask Slim to convince Candy to shoot his dog? How does Carlson justify the act?
Carlson asks Slim to convince Candy to shoot his dog because he feels like there is no reason for Candy to keep the dog alive. He justifies these feelings by describing the sorry state of the dog, addressing his smell, blindness, and inability to eat anything but milk—basically he says that the dog is better out of his misery because he is no longer young or useful and his quality of life is poor. Discuss with your students the issue of whether all things that are old and apparently useless should be discarded…and the reasons as to whether or not that applies to people. Would Carlson get rid of Slim, too?

3. "After a moment the ancient dog walked lamely in through the open door. He gazed about with mild, half-blind eyes. He sniffed, and then lay down and put his head between his paws. Curley popped into the doorway again and stood looking into the room. The dog raised his head, but when Curley jerked out, the grizzled head sank to the floor again."

a. What does Candy's dog symbolize?
In this book, Candy's dog is a symbol for weakness, and the natural decline that comes with age. The dog is old, sick, blind, and altogether unable to care for itself. When Carlson says that the dog should be killed and replaced with a new pup because of this, he is describing the attitude towards weak things on the ranch, which is that if they can't keep up, then they should be replaced.

b. One of the major conflicts explored in this chapter is man versus the natural world. How is that theme related to Candy's dog?
The natural world has taken a toll on Candy's dog. If it weren't for Candy spoon-feeding the dog milk, it would be unable to find food for itself and would die. But Candy keeps the dog alive despite the fact that it would die if left to the forces of nature, suggesting that man can combat nature, though the results may not be altogether positive.

c. How is the conflict of man versus the natural world related to Slim's dog, Lulu, and her pups?
In the case of Slim's dog, Lulu, and her pups, the reader sees the consequence of being weak in a situation with limited resources. Lulu is not able to make enough milk for all nine of the puppies that she births, so Slim is forced to eliminate some of them because there are not enough resources to go around. This relates to man because it shows that in a situation in which limited resources are available, only the strongest will survive, whereas the weakest will be eliminated just like the four pups that Slim had to drown (who would have likely died of starvation anyway).

Of Mice And Men Chapter 2
Reading Activity 7: Meaning and Inferences

Anchor Standard	8th Grade	9th-10th Grade
CCRA.R.1	RL.8.1	RL.9-10.1
CCRA.SL.1	SL.8.1	SL.9-10.1

Objective
Students will answer questions about selected passages from the text which require them to extract meaning or inferences from the text.

Directions
The following pages contain passages from Chapter 2 of *Of Mice and Men* and questions related to the passages that require close reading to answer. Students should answer the questions related to the passages.

This can be done as a whole-class activity, individually, or in small groups. If it is done individually or in small groups, come together as a class to discuss the answers to the questions.

Follow-Up/Assessment/Extension
Collect the worksheets for review and/or grading.

Of Mice And Men Chapter 2: Meaning & Inferences 1
Read the passages and answer the related questions.

1. *""Yeah? Married two weeks and got the eye? Maybe that's why Curley's pants is full of ants."*

What does the idiom "pants is full of ants" mean here, and what is its cause?

2. *""For two bits I'd shove out of here. If we can get jus' a few dollars in the poke we'll shove off and go up the American River and pan gold. We can make maybe a couple of dollars a day there, and we might hit a pocket."*

George consider this alternative plan when he recognizes that the ranch may be a potentially hostile place. Does he believe that it is actually possible? If so, why? If not, then why does he even mention it?

3. *"Well, Curley's pretty handy," the swamper said skeptically. "Never did seem right to me. S'pose Curley jumps a big guy an' licks him. Ever'body says what a game guy Curley is. And s'pose he does the same thing and gets licked. Then ever'body says the big guy oughtta pick on somebody his own size, and maybe they gang up on the big guy. Never did seem right to me. Seem like Curley ain't givin' nobody a chance."*

What does "givin' nobody a chance" mean?

4. *Slim looked through George and beyond him. "Ain't many guys travel around together," he mused. "I don't know why. Maybe ever'body in the whole damn world is scared of each other."*

What is Slim suggesting about "guys"? Why is "ever'body" significant?

5. *George said, "Ya know, Lennie, I'm scared I'm gonna tangle with that bastard myself. I hate his guts. Jesus Christ! Come on. They won't be a damn thing left to eat."*

Why does George respond so strongly to Curley?

Of Mice And Men Chapter 2: Meaning & Inferences 1 Suggested Answers

Read the passages and answer the related questions.

1. *""Yeah? Married two weeks and got the eye? Maybe that's why Curley's pants is full of ants."*

What does the idiom "pants is full of ants" mean here, and what is its cause?
In this case, the idiom "pants is full of ants" means "the reason why Curley is so thirsty to pick a fight". Curley's pants are full of ants because even though Curley just married his wife, she is already flirting and teasing other ranchers.

2. *""For two bits I'd shove out of here. If we can get jus' a few dollars in the poke we'll shove off and go up the American River and pan gold. We can make maybe a couple of dollars a day there, and we might hit a pocket."*

George considers this alternative plan when he recognizes that the ranch may be a potentially hostile place. Does he believe that it is actually possible? If so, why? If not, then why does he even mention it?
It has already been shown that George and Lennie make themselves feel better and safer by talking about a future where they do not have to face the issues that are currently plaguing them. The fact that George's hopeful talk about mining gold mirrors his talk about owning a farm with rabbits suggests to the reader that he does not actually believe this plan will come into fruition, but he talks about it nonetheless to make himself feel better.

3. *"Well, Curley's pretty handy," the swamper said skeptically. "Never did seem right to me. S'pose Curley jumps a big guy an' licks him. Ever'body says what a game guy Curley is. And s'pose he does the same thing and gets licked. Then ever'body says the big guy oughtta pick on somebody his own size, and maybe they gang up on the big guy. Never did seem right to me. Seem like Curley ain't givin' nobody a chance."*

What does "givin' nobody a chance" mean?
This means that no matter who Curley decides to pick on and no matter what the outcome of their fight is, Curley will come out on top in the eyes of the ranch. This is true because he can beat someone larger than him and be praised for being a great fighter, or he can lose to that same large person and the other person will be chastised for picking on someone smaller than him.

4. *Slim looked through George and beyond him. "Ain't many guys travel around together," he mused. "I don't know why. Maybe ever'body in the whole damn world is scared of each other."*

What is Slim suggesting about "guys"? Why is "ever'body" significant?
Slim is suggesting that "guys" keep to themselves and don't pair up or rely on other people like George and Lennie do because they are afraid of everyone else. It is significant that Slim says "ever'body" is like this because it shows just how different George and Lennie are for relying on each other.

Of Mice And Men Chapter 2: Meaning & Inferences 1 Suggested Answers Page 2

5. *George said, "Ya know, Lennie, I'm scared I'm gonna tangle with that bastard myself. I hate his guts. Jesus Christ! Come on. They won't be a damn thing left to eat."*

Why does George respond so strongly to Curley?
George responds so strongly to Curley because he is mad at how Curley threatened Lennie in such an unprovoked manner. George knows how innocent and peaceful Lennie is, and is therefore angered by Curley's attempts to persuade Lennie into getting in a fight with him. George finds Curley's behavior morally despicable.

Of Mice And Men Chapter 2: Meaning & Inferences 2

Read the passage and answer the related questions.

...He got married a couple of weeks ago. Wife lives over in the boss's house. Seems like Curley is cockier'n ever since he got married."
George grunted, "Maybe he's showin' off for his wife."
The swamper warmed to his gossip. "You seen that glove on his left hand?"
"Yeah. I seen it."
"Well, that glove's fulla vaseline."
"Vaseline? What the hell for?"
"Well, I tell ya what—Curley says he's keepin' that hand soft for his wife."
George studied the cards absorbedly. "That's a dirty thing to tell around," he said. The old man was reassured. He had drawn a derogatory statement from George. He felt safe now, and he spoke more confidently. "Wait'll you see Curley's wife."
George cut the cards again and put out a solitaire lay, slowly and deliberately. "Purty?" he asked casually.
"Yeah. Purty . . . . but—"
George studied his cards. "But what?"
"Well—she got the eye."
"Yeah? Married two weeks and got the eye? Maybe that's why Curley's pants is full of ants."
"I seen her give Slim the eye. Slim's a jerkline skinner. Hell of a nice fella. Slim don't need to wear no high-heeled boots on a grain team. I seen her give Slim the eye. Curley never seen it. An' I seen her give Carlson the eye."
George pretended a lack of interest. "Looks like we was gonna have fun."
The swamper stood up from his box. "Know what I think?" George did not answer. "Well, I think Curley's married . . . . a tart."

1. What is George's response to Curley's glove?

2. What does George's response suggest about his views towards sex?

3. Why does a "derogatory statement" reassure Candy?

4. What attribute is praiseworthy in Curley's wife? What does that suggest about society's view of women?

5. What is the effect of the comparison of Curley to Slim? Which is more optimally "masculine"?

Of Mice And Men Chapter 2: Meaning & Inferences 2 Suggested Answers

Read the passage and answer the related questions.

"…He got married a couple of weeks ago. Wife lives over in the boss's house. Seems like Curley is cockier'n ever since he got married."
George grunted, "Maybe he's showin' off for his wife."
The swamper warmed to his gossip. "You seen that glove on his left hand?"
"Yeah. I seen it."
"Well, that glove's fulla vaseline."
"Vaseline? What the hell for?"
"Well, I tell ya what—Curley says he's keepin' that hand soft for his wife."
George studied the cards absorbedly. "That's a dirty thing to tell around," he said. The old man was reassured. He had drawn a derogatory statement from George. He felt safe now, and he spoke more confidently. "Wait'll you see Curley's wife."
George cut the cards again and put out a solitaire lay, slowly and deliberately. "Purty?" he asked casually.
"Yeah. Purty . . . . but—"
George studied his cards. "But what?"
"Well—she got the eye."
"Yeah? Married two weeks and got the eye? Maybe that's why Curley's pants is full of ants."
"I seen her give Slim the eye. Slim's a jerkline skinner. Hell of a nice fella. Slim don't need to wear no high-heeled boots on a grain team. I seen her give Slim the eye. Curley never seen it. An' I seen her give Carlson the eye."
George pretended a lack of interest. "Looks like we was gonna have fun."
The swamper stood up from his box. "Know what I think?" George did not answer. "Well, I think Curley's married . . . . a tart."

1. What is important about George's response to Candy's statement about Curley's glove?
George says, "That's a dirty thing to tell around." This is a middle-of-the-road comment that shows he knows it isn't proper to go around talking about people's private business yet leaves the door open to hear more.

2. What does George's response tell us about his character?
George keeps a "poker face" with regard to the gossip Candy tells him. He chooses to appear not particularly interested in what Candy says, so he doesn't get tangled up in the relationships. He is careful about his responses so as not to appear either "with" or "against" any party involved. This scene combined with the advice George has already given Lennie shows George as a man who doesn't want trouble; he just wants to work and be free to live his own life.

3. Why does a "derogatory statement" reassure Candy?
George's response let Candy know George wouldn't get him in trouble for talking about Curley's and his wife. He therefore felt reassured to go on and tell more.

4. What Curley's wife's most significant attribute? What is a "tart"?
Curley's wife's flirtatiousness is her most significant attribute in this book. A "tart" is a promiscuous woman.

5. What is George's interest in the gossip about Curley's wife? What is Candy's?
George's interest is guarded curiosity; almost like he's gathering intelligence and identifying possible threats to himself and Lennie. The actions of Curley's wife give Candy something to gossip about, something to talk about with the "new guy" at the ranch. He doesn't seem to have a particular interest in Curley's wife, so much as he enjoys observing and talking about her.

Of Mice And Men Chapter 2
Writing Activity 1: What Is Masculinity?

Anchor Standard	8th Grade	9th-10th Grade
CCRA.SL.1	SL.8.1, 1a-1d	SL.9-10.1, 1a-1d
CCRA.SL.3	SL.8.4	SL.9-10.4
CCRA.W.1	W.8.2	W.9-10.2
CCRA.W.2	W.8.4	W.9-10.4
CCRA.W.4	W.8.5	W.9-10.5
CCRA.W.5		W.9-10.7
		W.9-10.9, 9b

Objectives
- Students will evaluate and analyze textual evidence to define the concept of masculinity within the parameters of the novel.
- Students will evaluate passages that reveal characterization, motive and conflict.
- Students will examine language for ways in which characterization, motive and conflict illuminate the definition of masculinity presented in the novel.
- Students will write a composition in which they consider their analysis of relevant passages to answer the question, "What is masculinity?"

Directions
The following series of worksheets and information organizers can be used by students individually, in small groups, or done partly as a whole-class activity. They are intended to guide students through the process of reading and thinking critically about information by ultimately answering the single question, "What is masculinity?"

Preview the following pages. Determine the best way to have your particular class handle this assignment (individually, pairs, groups, whole-class, or some combination). A combination of group work (to do the analyzing of the text on the chart page) followed by individual work (to do the second and third pages of the assignment) would most likely be best to fulfill the standards listed for this assignment.

Follow-Up/Assessment/Extension
- The written assignment will be a good basis for assessment of the students' success with this assignment. Create a rubric explaining the criteria on which their written assignments will be evaluated.
- Tell students to continue observing examples of how masculinity is expressed and what versions of it are valued.
- Have some students read/present their writing assignments to the class to practice more speaking/listening skills and to expose all students to each others' ideas.
- Use this assignment to introduce the themes of masculinity, authority and isolation.

Of Mice And Men Chapter 2: What Is Masculinity?

In chapters 2, masculinity as a concept is explored primarily through comparisons of Curley and Slim, as well as other minor characters.

The ways in which characters interact fuel a narrative by advancing conflict, and therefore, plot. *Of Mice and Men* is very much a novel about masculine identity, competition and status. This is apparent in how the men interact with one another.

Using textual evidence from chapter 2, look for patterns to begin formulating an answer to the question "What is masculinity?". As you develop an answer, consider how it relates to emerging conflicts and why it is significant. What do these relationship dynamics reveal about the characters? How do they define the concept of masculinity in the novel?

To determine an idea about how masculinity is defined within the novel:

1. Identify passages and quotes where Curley and Slim are described and in which they interact with other male characters.

2. Examine the context of your quotes.

3. Consider the connotation and denotation of key phrases in your quotes.

    a. What is the tone—friendly, adversarial, angry, competitive?
    b. Is there a conflict?
    c. What attitudes about masculinity are the characters revealing or concealing in their language?

4. Look for patterns in your evidence. Is a word or idea repeated? Use these patterns to shape an answer to the question.

Of Mice And Men Chapter 2: What Is Masculinity?

Complete the chart to analyze information to develop ideas to write your essay.

Character	Quote/Passage	Observations	What does it express about masculinity?
Curley Passage 1			
Curley Passage 2			
Curley Passage 3			

Slim Passage 1			
Slim Passage 2			
Slim Passage 3			

Of Mice And Men Chapter 2: What Is Masculinity?

Evaluate Your Textual Evidence

1. Are there any similarities between Curley and Slim?

2. What are the primary differences between Curley and Slim?

3. How do other people perceive each, Curley and Slim?

4. How do others perceive the masculinity of Curley and Slim? Are those perceptions positive or negative?

Of Mice And Men Chapter 2
Suggested Writing Assignments

Anchor Standard	8th Grade	9th-10th Grade
CCRA.W.1	W.8.1, 1a-1d	W.9-10.1, 1a-1e
CCRA.W.2	W.8.2, 2a-2f	W.9-10.2, 2a-2f
CCRA.W.3	W.8.3, 3a-3e	W.9-10.3, 3a-3e
CCRA.W.4	W.8.4	W.9-10.4
CCRA.W.5	W.8.5	W.9-10.5

Objective
Students will be assigned or will choose one of a selection of writing assignments pertaining to Chapter 2 of *Of Mice and Men* to fulfill one or more of the standards listed above.

Directions
To provide you with maximum flexibility for differentiated instruction, the following page has a list of suggested writing assignments, all related to Chapter 2 of *Of Mice and Men*. Either assign individual students particular assignments to do or allow students to choose their own assignments.

A second page of "Quick Write" topics is also included.

Follow-Up/Assessment/Extension
- Have dramatic readings of students' narratives or poems.
- Create a "reading room" space in your classroom where students can donate their writing assignments for others in the class to read.
- Allow students to do more than one assignment if they want to.
- Use the "left-over" assignments (not chosen for this activity) as topics for journal entries.

Of Mice And Men Chapter 2: Creative Analytical Writing Assignments

1. Write a description of George and Lennie from the boss' perspective.
2. Write a scene in dialogue of the conversation that morning between the boss and Crooks.
3. What are the "rules" of gossiping?
4. Write a letter from Curley's wife to her family who live far away.
5. Write guidelines for living in the bunkhouse.
6. Write a description of Curley's boxing career.
7. Write a scene in dialogue of the conversation between Slim and Candy about putting down Candy's dog.
8. Write a paragraph that speculates why George feels so much anger.
9. Write a flashback scene of Curley's wedding.
10. Describe how Lennie and George benefit from traveling together.

Of Mice And Men Chapter 2: Quick-Write Writing Assignments

1. Who is the better dog owner, Candy or Slim?
2. What lies does George tell? Are they justified?
3. Why is it fitting that George plays solitaire?
4. Why is the use of nicknames significant?
5. Why is Lennie "fascinated" by Curley's wife?
6. What events might be foreshadowed in this chapter?
7. How are the men compared to animals? Why is the comparison significant?
8. Consider George asking Lennie to remember their camping location as a future hiding place. What do you suspect might happen?
9. Comment on Lennie's dishonesty.
10. Comment on Lennie's remorse and willingness to live in a cave.

NOTES
OF MICE AND MEN

MATERIALS: CHAPTER 3
OF MICE AND MEN

Reading Activity 1: True or False?

Reading Activity 2: Analyzing Passages

Reading Activity 3: Foil Character Study

Reading Activity 4: Action, Character, Decision

Reading Activity 5: Figurative Language

Reading Activity 6: Elements of Fiction & Literary Devices

Reading Activity 7: Meaning and Inferences

Writing Activity 1: How Is Strength Or Weakness Determined?

Suggested Writing Assignments

Quick-Write Assignments

NOTES
OF MICE AND MEN

Of Mice And Men Chapter 3
Reading Activity 1: True or False

Anchor Standard	8th Grade	9th-10th Grade
CCRA.R.1	RL.8.1	RL.9-10.1
CCRA.SL.1	SL.8.1	SL.9-10.1
CCRA.SL.4	SL.8.4	SL.9-10.4

Objectives
- Students will be able to cite the parts of the text that support their analysis of what the text says or infers.
- Students will consider statements about the text, determine whether those statements are true or false, and will give textual evidence supporting their choices.
- Students will work together in small groups to discuss, analyze, and evaluate the statements made.
- Students will evaluate the analytical work of their peers.

Directions
Prior to reading Chapter 3: Give students (or post) the following list of statements about the chapters, and explain to students that they should read Chapter 3 to find out if these statements are true or false:

> Slim is impressed by Lennie's physical strength.
> George lies to Slim about what happens in Weed.
> George is interested in hiring a prostitute.
> Candy already has half the money needed to buy a small farm.
> George gives Lennie permission to hit Curley.
> Curley accidentally mangles his hand in a machine.

After reading Chapter 3: The worksheets on the following pages can be done by students individually, in small groups, or as a whole class. Below are directions to use the questions as a group activity to fulfill more state standards:

- Cut the worksheet apart, making each question and answer box a slip.
- Divide your class into six groups and give one question and a True/False evaluation form to each group. Tell students they are to discuss the statement and determine if the statement is true or false, supporting their decision with evidence from the text. Tell them their answers will be evaluated on the criteria given on the evaluation form.
- Give students ample time to discuss the statements and record their answers.
- Have the groups swap True or False question slips so that each group can evaluate another group's answer. The group should fill in the number of the question they are evaluating, decide how well the answer fulfills the criteria listed, and fill out the form accordingly.
- Repeat the previous step until all the groups have evaluated each others' answers.
- Collect the evaluations and answer slips.

Follow-Up/Assessment/Extension:

- You could average and record the grades each group received for its answers.
- Students could write in their journals or notebooks one thing they learned from this activity.
- You could hold a whole-class discussion about each or any of the statements, either solely orally or using a blank True or False Worksheet on your whiteboard, filling it in as the discussion unfolds.
- At the beginning of the next class, you could hold a brief discussion reviewing the facts addressed by the True/False Worksheet, to see what students have retained and to reinforce the information.
- You could have students make up (and fill in) their own True/False Worksheets for other information located within this chapter.

Of Mice And Men Chapter 3: True or False?

Write *True* or *False* in the blank next to each statement. Below the statement, explain why you chose true or false, referencing the text to support your choices.

_____ 1. Slim is impressed by Lennie's physical strength.

_____ 2. George lies to Slim about what happens in Weed.

_____ 3. George is interested in hiring a prostitute.

Of Mice And Men Chapter 3 True or False? Page 2

_____ 4. Candy already has half the money needed to buy a small farm.

_____ 5. George gives Lennie permission to hit Curley.

_____ 6. Curley accidentally mangles his hand in a machine.

Of Mice And Men Chapter 3 True or False? Evaluation

List Your Group's Members: Your Group's Question # _____

_____   _____   _____

_____   _____   _____

1 = No, Not At All **2** = A Little **3** = Some **4** = Yes **5** = Yes, Very Well

Evaluation of Question # ___
Does the explanation support the answer of true or false?   1 2 3 4 5
Is there good textual evidence to support the answer?   1 2 3 4 5
Is the answer clearly stated?   1 2 3 4 5
                    Total Score _____ of a possible 15 points

Evaluation of Question # ___
Does the explanation support the answer of true or false?   1 2 3 4 5
Is there good textual evidence to support the answer?   1 2 3 4 5
Is the answer clearly stated?   1 2 3 4 5
                    Total Score _____ of a possible 15 points

Evaluation of Question # ___
Does the explanation support the answer of true or false?   1 2 3 4 5
Is there good textual evidence to support the answer?   1 2 3 4 5
Is the answer clearly stated?   1 2 3 4 5
                    Total Score _____ of a possible 15 points

Evaluation of Question # ___
Does the explanation support the answer of true or false?   1 2 3 4 5
Is there good textual evidence to support the answer?   1 2 3 4 5
Is the answer clearly stated?   1 2 3 4 5
                    Total Score _____ of a possible 15 points

Evaluation of Question # ___
Does the explanation support the answer of true or false?   1 2 3 4 5
Is there good textual evidence to support the answer?   1 2 3 4 5
Is the answer clearly stated?   1 2 3 4 5
                    Total Score _____ of a possible 15 points

Of Mice And Men Chapter 3: True or False? Suggested Answers

Write *True* or *False* in the blank next to each statement. Below the statement, explain why you chose true or false, referencing the text to support your choices.

TRUE 1. Slim is impressed by Lennie's physical strength.

> He says that he never saw anyone as strong as Lennie and that no one could keep up with him working in the field. He is not exaggerating, which suggests that Lennie is indeed unusually strong.

FALSE 2. George lies to Slim about what happens in Weed.

> Slim is "quiet" and "calm," which allows George to relax enough to talk about the misunderstanding and troubles that occurred in Weed. George's conversation with Slim is confessional. It is clear that George needed to unburden himself of guilt and troubles, and Slim (described with "Godlike eyes") listens without judging.

FALSE 3. George is interested in hiring a prostitute.

> Unlike most ranchers, George is not interested in the services of a prostitute. He is clear that his goal is to save money, not spend it, though he adds that he might go along and have a drink.

TRUE 4. Candy already has half the money needed to buy a small farm.

> Yes, Candy has had steady employment and a disbursement of funds as compensation for the farming accident that took his hand. Candy's savings make the dream of purchasing a farm truly viable for the first time.

Of Mice And Men Chapter 3 True or False? Suggested Answers Page 2

TRUE 5. George gives Lennie permission to hit Curley.

> Despite George's earlier warnings to avoid Curley, George has correctly assessed that Curley has goaded Lennie into the physical altercation and that doing so was wrong. During the whole bewildering ordeal, Lennie looks to George for guidance. Finally he yells for Lennie to get him, and he repeats it.

FALSE 6. Curley accidentally mangles his hand in a machine.

> This is the cover story that the fair and moral Slim forces Curley to accept. Slim threatens to out Curley's cowardice and lack of character to the men of the ranch if he tells anyone the truth of what transpired or if he fires George and Lennie, who are victims of Curley's macho ignorance and cruelty.

Of Mice And Men Chapter 3
Reading Activity 2: Analyzing Passages

Anchor Standard	8th Grade	9th-10th Grade
CCRA.R.6	RL.8.1	RL.9-10.1
	RL.8.3	
	RL.8.4	RL.9-10.4
	RL.8.6	
CCRA.SL.1	SL.8.1	SL.9-10.1

Objectives
- Students will analyze what the text says explicitly as well as inferences drawn from the text.
- Students will analyze how different points of view of the characters and the audience (or reader) creates suspense or humor.
- Students will analyze the impact of specific word choices on meaning and tone.

Directions
On the pages that follow, there are 8 passages to analyze, each with a question or questions to guide the process. There are many ways to use these questions:

- You could use them as a worksheet for all students to complete individually.
- You could use the worksheet as your guide in a whole-class discussion. Have students turn to the first passage in the book, read it, then ask the question(s) orally. Repeat through all 8 questions.
- You could assign one passage to each of 8 different groups of students, for the students to discuss and come up with responses to the question(s). Then hold a whole-class discussion.
- You could read the passage and then see which student can find the passage first (to practice skimming skills). Then follow up with the questions(s) and discussion.
- You could have students choose one or two questions to respond to in writing in their notebooks or journals.

Follow-Up/Assessment/Extension
- Have students write about how the decision was made to put down Candy's dog. Did Candy agree? What evidence is there of his attitude toward it?
- Have students pick out other passages in this chapter that show interesting word usage, descriptions, or lack of clarity.
- As an introduction to this activity and this chapter, ask students to write about how groups make decisions. Is it possible to come to fair conclusions?

Of Mice And Men Chapter 3 Analyzing Passages

Answer the questions following the quotations completely.

1. George carefully built his line of solitaire cards. "Well, that girl rabbits in an' tells the law she been raped. The guys in Weed start a party out to lynch Lennie.

So we sit in a irrigation ditch under water all the rest of that day. Got on'y our heads sticking outa water, an' up under the grass that sticks out from the side of the ditch. An' that night we scrammed outa there."

What does the word "rabbits" probably mean here? Why is it significant?

2. The skinner had been studying the old dog with his calm eyes. "Yeah," he said. "You can have a pup if you want to." He seemed to shake himself free for speech. "Carl's right, Candy. That dog ain't no good to himself. I wisht somebody'd shoot me if I get old an' a cripple."

Why is the word "cripple" significant? Why is it significant that Slim says this to Candy?

3. Whit laid down his cards impressively. "Well, stick around an' keep your eyes open. You'll see plenty. She ain't concealin' nothing. I never seen nobody like her. She got the eye goin' all the time on everybody. I bet she even gives the stable buck the eye. I don't know what the hell she wants."

What references are made to eyes here? What does this suggest about eyes and seeing? How does gender factor in?

4. They fell into a silence. They looked at one another, amazed. This thing they had never really believed in was coming true. George said reverently, "Jesus Christ! I bet we could swing her." His eyes were full of wonder. "I bet we could swing her," he repeated softly.

What is happening with pronouns here? What does that suggest about George's view of the world?

Of Mice And Men Chapter 3 Analyzing Passages Page 2

5. Slim said, "Well, you been askin' me too often. I'm gettin' God damn sick of it. If you can't look after your own God damn wife, what you expect me to do about it? You lay offa me."

What is Slim suggesting that Curley is implying? Why is the repetition of "God damn" significant?

6. Carlson laughed. "You God damn punk," he said. "You tried to throw a scare into Slim, an' you couldn't make it stick. Slim throwed a scare into you. You're yella as a frog belly. I don't care if you're the best welter in the country. You come for me, an' I'll kick your God damn head off."

Why is Carlson emboldened? What is Carlson suggesting about power and authority?

7. Lennie covered his face with his huge paws and bleated with terror. He cried, "Make 'um stop, George." Then Curley attacked his stomach and cut off his wind.

What is the significance of the animal imagery? Does it make Lennie seem more forceful or less?

8. George turned to Lennie. "It ain't your fault," he said. "You don't need to be scairt no more. You done jus' what I tol' you to. Maybe you better go in the wash room an' clean up your face. You look like hell."

Does George accept responsibility for Lennie's actions? How is that conveyed in the text?

Of Mice And Men Chapter 3 Analyzing Passages Suggested Answers

Answer the questions following the quotations completely.

1. George carefully built his line of solitaire cards. "Well, that girl rabbits in an' tells the law she been raped. The guys in Weed start a party out to lynch Lennie.

So we sit in a irrigation ditch under water all the rest of that day. Got on'y our heads sticking outa water, an' up under the grass that sticks out from the side of the ditch. An' that night we scrammed outa there."

What does the word "rabbits" probably mean here? Why is it significant?
The word is being used in a colloquial and slang way. Here it likely means to go to or "hop to" quickly, as in the way a rabbit moves, The word rabbit has many connotations and related idioms (for example, a dead rabbit referring to pregnancy and a rabbit punch being dangerous and cowardly), but it directly relates to Lennie's main object of desire, which is threatened by incidents like the one that happened in Weed.

2. The skinner had been studying the old dog with his calm eyes. "Yeah," he said. "You can have a pup if you want to." He seemed to shake himself free for speech. "Carl's right, Candy. That dog ain't no good to himself. I wisht somebody'd shoot me if I get old an' a cripple."

Why is the word "cripple" significant? Why is it significant that Slim says this to Candy?
Slim is referring to the dog, but he might as well be referring to Candy, who has no hand at the end of his arm because of a terrible accident. By the transitive property, Slim is saying these things about Candy. Slim is also comparing an animal's life to a human's and judging them as equal.

3. Whit laid down his cards impressively. "Well, stick around an' keep your eyes open. You'll see plenty. She ain't concealin' nothing. I never seen nobody like her. She got the eye goin' all the time on everybody. I bet she even gives the stable buck the eye. I don't know what the hell she wants."

What references are made to eyes here? What does this suggest about eyes and seeing? How does gender factor in?
Words like "eye" and "concealing" and "seen" all highlight the idea of looking at something or being looked at. What is at issue in the men's gossip is which is acceptable: being looked at or looking. The men clearly look at her—Whit says "keep your eyes open," but reject her "giv[ing] the eye." Men are free to look at women, but the opposite is considered taboo.

4. They fell into a silence. They looked at one another, amazed. This thing they had never really believed in was coming true. George said reverently, "Jesus Christ! I bet we could swing her." His eyes were full of wonder. "I bet we could swing her," he repeated softly.

What is happening with pronouns here? What does that suggest about George's view of the world?
In a book devoid of many female characters, the dream—once unattainable—is gendered female: "I bet we could swing her." It aligns property with things that are female—like a wife or prostitutes, all which can be had by men with money. The dream of a ranch almost becomes a substitute for dreaming of having a family, a wife, which seems out of the question.

Of Mice and Men Analyzing Passages Page 3

5. Slim said, "Well, you been askin' me too often. I'm gettin' God damn sick of it. If you can't look after your own God damn wife, what you expect me to do about it? You lay offa me."

What is Slim suggesting that Curley is implying? Why is the repetition of "God damn" significant?
Slim has repeatedly been depicted as a Godlike character—moral and just and fair. Here Curley implies that Slim may have committed adultery with his wife. Slim, normally calm and unperturbed, repeats the phrase "God damn." Here it functions as a moral judgment and can be taken almost literally, as in God judges Curley for his errant behavior and treatment of people.

6. Carlson laughed. "You God damn punk," he said. "You tried to throw a scare into Slim, an' you couldn't make it stick. Slim throwed a scare into you. You're yella as a frog belly. I don't care if you're the best welter in the country. You come for me, an' I'll kick your God damn head off."

Why is Carlson emboldened? What is Carlson suggesting about power and authority?
Slim provides moral authority over Curley, and Carlson is quick to join Slim in that domination (as long as Slim is taking the lead). Carlson—and Steinbeck—suggest that authority is not determined solely by position or class, as Curley is the boss' son, and more well off than ranch workers. Instead, true power comes from behaving nobly and morally.

7. Lennie covered his face with his huge paws and bleated with terror. He cried, "Make 'um stop, George." Then Curley attacked his stomach and cut off his wind.

What is the significance of the animal imagery? Does it make Lennie seem more forceful or less?
Lennie seems pathetic and scared, which runs opposite to his natural strength. Like an animal ("paws" and "bleated"), Lennie is acutely unaware of the pettiness that motivates Curley to attack him; all he knows is that he is being "attacked." "Paws" repeat the bear-like imagery, but goats "bleat," perhaps referencing sacrificial goats.

8. George turned to Lennie. "It ain't your fault," he said. "You don't need to be scairt no more. You done jus' what I tol' you to. Maybe you better go in the wash room an' clean up your face. You look like hell."

Does George accept responsibility for Lennie's actions? How is that conveyed in the text?
He does to some extent; at least that he absolves Lennie of any guilt. Since Lennie cannot understand the subtleties of the interaction with Curley, George gives him a contextual frame for understanding what happened ("you done jus'...") and reassures him ("don't need to be scairt"). He also offers parental guidance ("clean up your face"), showing that he ultimately takes responsibility for Lennie.

Of Mice and Men Chapter 3
Reading Activity 3: Foil Character Study

Anchor Standard	8th Grade	9th-10th Grade
CCRA.R.1	RL.8.1	RL.9-10.1
CCRA.SL.1	SL.8.1	SL.9-10.1

Objective
Using textual evidence, students will explore how characters can act as foils to reveal more significant information about a protagonist.

Directions
The Foil Character Study worksheet on the following page could be used in many ways, completed by small groups of students, individual students, or as a whole class activity.

Students will be able to identify how details about characters serve an additional function of revealing information about a protagonist.

Students may (and should) use their books to skim through the chapters to refresh their memories or gather more information about the characters.

After students complete the worksheets discuss students' answers as a whole class. Collect the worksheets for grading, if you choose, or have students put them in their notebooks for further study.

Follow-Up/Assessment/Extension
Revisit this assignment later in the unit and compare the way that Curley reacts when Lennie kills Curley's wife.

Of Mice And Men Chapter 3 Reading Activity 3: Foil Character Study

Complete the chart below with quotes from the text and inferences about Lennie and Curley. Consider how Curley's attributes and actions provide insight into Lennie's character.

Incident	Quotes/Phrases	What does this show about Curley?	What does this show about Lennie?
When George questions Lennie about seeing Curley's wife in the barn			
When Curley asks Lennie what he is laughing at			
When Curley strikes Lennie			
When Lennie is holding and damaging Curley's hand			

Of Mice And Men Chapter 3
Reading Activity 3: Foil Character Study Suggested Answers

Complete the chart below with quotes from the text and inferences about Lennie and Curley. Consider how Curley's attributes and actions provide insight into Lennie's character.

Incident	Quotes/Phrases	What does this show about Curley?	What does this show about Lennie?
When George questions Lennie about seeing Curley's wife in the barn	Selection may vary	Generally that George believes that Curley can't control his wife and she represents a danger to Lennie.	Lennie is unaware of people manipulating him and he is very innocent and preoccupied with his puppy. This conversation is juxtaposed with Lennie recalling that Slim has warned him against petting the puppy too hard (a foreshadowing).
When Curley asks Lennie what he is laughing at	Selection may vary	Curley does not imagine that the look on Lennie's face is about anything other than Curley—he is self-absorbed and always looking for a fight. He'll use any reason to justify becoming aggressive.	Lennie is not quick-witted enough to defend himself.
When Curley strikes Lennie	Selection may vary	Curley is an experienced boxer, and that is apparent from the description of his physical movements.	Lennie is child-like and positively terrified and bewildered that Curley has attacked him.
When Lennie is holding and damaging Curley's hand	Selection may vary	Curley loses any control in the situation and is helpless, "flopping like a fish on a line."	Lennie is unusually strong, so strong that he can inflict severe damage with little deliberate effort.

Of Mice And Men Chapter 3
Reading Activity 4: Action, Character, Decision

Anchor Standard	8th Grade	9th-10th Grade
CCRA.R.1	RL.8.3	
CCRA.SL.1	SL.8.1	SL.9-10.1

Objective
Students will identify whether particular lines of dialogue or incidents in the story propel the action, reveal aspects of a character, or provoke a decision.

Directions
The following page contains passages from Chapter 3 of Of Mice and Men. Students should determine whether the passages advance the action, reveal aspects of a character, or provoke a decision.
This can be done as a whole-class activity, individually, or in small groups.

Follow-Up/Assessment/Extension
Have students skim Chapter 3 to find one example of a passage that propels the action, one that reveals aspects of a character, and one that provokes a decision. Again, this could be done individually or as a group.

Of Mice And Men Chapter 3: Action, Character, Decision

Write **A** (for Action) **C** (for Character) or **D** (for Decision) in the blank next to each to identify whether the passage/statement advances the action, tells us more about a character, or provokes a decision. On the lines under each question, provide a short explanation of your choice.

___ 1. "Well, I can't stand him in here," said Carlson. "That stink hangs around even after he's gone." He walked over with his heavy-legged stride and looked down at the dog. "Got no teeth," he said. "He's all stiff with rheumatism. He ain't no good to you, Candy. An' he ain't no good to himself. Why'n't you shoot him, Candy?"

___ 2. Candy looked for help from face to face.

___ 3. Then he said thoughtfully, "Look, if me an' Lennie work a month an' don't spen' nothing, we'll have a hunderd bucks. That'd be four fifty. I bet we could swing her for that. Then you an' Lennie could go get her started an' I'd get a job an' make up the res', an' you could sell eggs an' stuff like that."

___ 4. "I ought to of shot that dog myself, George. I shouldn't ought to of let no stranger shoot my dog."

___ 5. Lennie was still smiling with delight at the memory of the ranch.

Of Mice And Men Chapter 3:
Action, Character, Decision Suggested Answers

Write **A** (for Action) **C** (for Character) or **D** (for Decision) in the blank next to each to identify whether the passage/statement advances the action, tells us more about a character, or provokes a decision. On the lines under each question, provide a short explanation of your choice.

A 1. "Well, I can't stand him in here," said Carlson. "That stink hangs around even after he's gone." He walked over with his heavy-legged stride and looked down at the dog. "Got no teeth," he said. "He's all stiff with rheumatism. He ain't no good to you, Candy. An' he ain't no good to himself. Why'n't you shoot him, Candy?"
Carlson's direct question to Candy creates conflict, which fuels action and the development of plot. Candy does not want to kill his pet, but Carlson is indifferent to the value of the animal's life.

A 2. Candy looked for help from face to face.
Candy searches for an ally to support sparing the dog's life. No one supports him, despite his apparent grief.

D 3. Then he said thoughtfully, "Look, if me an' Lennie work a month an' don't spen' nothing, we'll have a hunderd bucks. That'd be four fifty. I bet we could swing her for that. Then you an' Lennie could go get her started an' I'd get a job an' make up the res', an' you could sell eggs an' stuff like that."
This is a moment when it actually dawns on George that his dream might actually be within reach. He shifts his thinking and makes a decision to believe in the dream.

C 4. "I ought to of shot that dog myself, George. I shouldn't ought to of let no stranger shoot my dog."
Like his name, Candy's remorse shows him to be sweet and kind. He recognizes that no one else cared about his dog the way he did, and to allow someone without a personal connection to the dog to take its life does not show loyalty or care.

A 5. Lennie was still smiling with delight at the memory of the ranch.
Here Curley finds a lame excuse to pick a fight—that Lennie is appearing to laugh at him. It shows how self-centered Curley is and how he is an opportunist when it comes to creating situations where he can prove his masculinity at the expense of others.

Of Mice And Men Chapter 3
Reading Activity 5: Figurative Language

Anchor Standard	8th Grade	9th-10th Grade
CCRA.R.4	RL.8.4	RL.9-10.4
CCRA.SL.1	SL.8.1	SL.9-10.1

Objectives
- Students will determine the meaning of words and phrases as they are used in the text, and how hyperbole and understatement creates meaning.
- Students will determine how figurative language contributes to meaning.

Directions
The following page has a passage from the text which includes examples of figurative language. This work-sheet can be done individually, as a whole-class activity, or in small groups. Discuss the answers as a whole class. Collect the worksheets and record the grades if you choose to do so.

Follow-Up/Assessment/Extension
Ask students to begin tracking instances of a particular type of figurative language (personification, metaphor, hyperbole, etc.) in the text. Ask students to make a list to track their observations. Assign students a paper that uses these examples to make an argument about how the language creates meaning.

Of Mice And Men Chapter 3: Figurative Language

Read the following passages and determine if the passage contains hyperbole (H) or understatement (U). On the lines below, explain how figurative language creates meaning in the passage.

_____1. Maybe we'd have a cow or a goat, and the cream is so God damn thick you got to cut it with a knife and take it out with a spoon.

_____2. "We could live offa the fatta the lan'."

_____3. "It wasn't nothing," said Slim. "I would of had to drowned most of 'em anyways. No need to thank me about that."

_____4. That's right. You couldn't find it in a hundred years.

_____5. You jus' let 'em try to get the rabbits. I'll break their God damn necks. I'll . . . . I'll smash 'em with a stick." He subsided, grumbling to himself, threatening the future cats which might dare to disturb the future rabbits.

Of Mice And Men Chapter 3: Figurative Language Suggested Answers

Read the following passages and determine if the passage contains hyperbole (H) or understatement (U). On the lines below, explain how figurative language creates meaning in the passage.

H 1. Maybe we'd have a cow or a goat, and the cream is so God damn thick you got to cut it with a knife and take it out with a spoon.
Here the story that George has repeated so many times to delight Lennie is exaggerated, which shows how badly and how deeply they wish the dream would come true. They care about these details because they provide comfort.

H 2. "We could live offa the fatta the lan'."
The statement suggests that they could be fully self-sufficient and self-sustaining to have total and complete personal freedom. This is a wishful exaggeration.

U 3. "It wasn't nothing," said Slim. "I would of had to drowned most of 'em anyways. No need to thank me about that."
Slim does not realize that he has fulfilled one of Lennie's long-held dreams by gifting him a puppy. He literally does mean that the gift is nothing to him, as he would have killed the puppies.

H 4. That's right. You couldn't find it in a hundred years.
George says this to Candy as they talk about the men's dream of obtaining a farm. He becomes protective of his dream with Lennie and effectively shuts Candy out, saying that he could never find an adequate farm for $600.

H 5. You jus' let 'em try to get the rabbits. I'll break their God damn necks. I'll . . . . I'll smash 'em with a stick." He subsided, grumbling to himself, threatening the future cats which might dare to disturb the future rabbits.
Lennie is so excited about his dream that he defends it against any encroachment—here he exaggerates (one hopes) the physical force he would use against cats that might harm his rabbits.

Of Mice And Men Chapter 3
Reading Activity 6: Elements of Fiction & Literary Devices

Anchor Standard	8th Grade	9th-10th Grade
CCRA.R.1	RL.8.1	RL.9-10.1
	RL.8.2	RL.9-10.2
	RL.8.3	RL.9-10.4
	RL.8.4	RL.9-10.5
	RL.8.6	
CCRA.SL.1	SL.8.1	SL.9-10.1

Objective
Students will study and discuss passages from the text to examine symbol, motif and theme and explore how these create meaning in the text.

Directions
Use the following discussion questions as a guide to discussing symbol, motif and theme, in these chapters. You can give students the questions ahead of time and have them formulate answers prior to the class discussion or you can jump right in with a whole class discussion without student preparation if your students will handle that well.

As you hold the class discussion, be sure to include conversations defining symbol, motif and theme and explaining how these work together to advance meaning in the text.

Follow-Up/Assessment/Extension
After your discussion, ask students to look for recurrences of these symbols, motifs and themes in future chapters.

Of Mice And Men Chapter 3: Elements of Fiction & Literary Devices

Read the following passages and answer questions, making inferences about the significance of symbols, motifs and themes.

1. "Although there was evening brightness showing through the windows of the bunk house, inside it was dusk."

The chapter opens with a reference to a motif of darkness, which is repeated multiple times through the chapter. What is the effect of the motif?

2. "George looked over at Slim and saw the calm, Godlike eyes fastened on him."

The description of Slim's eyes as "Godlike" suggests what about him?

3. George said, "You get right up an' take this pup back to the nest. He's gotta sleep with his mother. You want to kill him? Just born last night an' you take him out of the nest. You take him back or I'll tell Slim not to let you have him."

How does this example fit with a larger theme of protecting the weak?

4. "It was obvious that Whit was not interested in his cards. He laid his hand down and George scooped it in. George laid out his deliberate solitaire hand—seven cards and six on top, and five on top of those."

How does the failed euchre game with Whit relate to the theme of companionship/isolation?

Of Mice And Men Chapter 3: Elements of Fiction & Literary Devices Page 2

5. "…Susy's got nice chairs to set in, too. If a guy don't want a flop, why he can just set in the chairs and have a couple or three shots and pass the time of day and Susy don't give a damn. She ain't rushin' guys through and kickin' 'em out if they don't want a flop…."

…

"Me an' Lennie's rollin' up a stake," said George. "I might go in an' set and have a shot, but I ain't puttin' out no two and a half."

…

George sighed. "You give me a good whore house every time," he said. "A guy can go in an' get drunk and get ever'thing outta his system all at once, an' no messes. And he knows how much it's gonna set him back. There here jail baits is just set on the trigger of the hoosegow."

Consider Whit's description of whorehouses and George's response, as well as George's reminder to Lennie about Andy Cushman. What is being suggested by the text about women?

_____
_____
_____
_____

Of Mice And Men Chapter 3:
Elements of Fiction & Literary Devices Suggested Answers

Read the following passages and answer questions, making inferences about the significance of symbols, motifs and themes.

1. "Although there was evening brightness showing through the windows of the bunk house, inside it was dusk."

The chapter opens with a reference to a motif of darkness, which is repeated multiple times through the chapter. What is the effect of the motif?
The darkness of the bunk makes it seem like a foreboding and dangerous place, which it becomes in this chapter as Curley attacks Lennie. The patterns of dark and light are also part of the cyclical aspect of nature and time, which is also present in the novel.

2. "George looked over at Slim and saw the calm, Godlike eyes fastened on him."

The description of Slim's eyes as "Godlike" suggests what about him?
He is definitely different than the other men. His "gravity" suggests seriousness and moral authority that the other men do not necessarily exhibit. Slim is a natural leader of men, and he is quietly intuitive and non-judgmental. George—who constantly tells Lennie not to talk—ultimately confesses his feeling about Lennie and the event in Weed to Slim.

3. George said, "You get right up an' take this pup back to the nest. He's gotta sleep with his mother. You want to kill him? Just born last night an' you take him out of the nest. You take him back or I'll tell Slim not to let you have him."

How does this example fit with a larger theme of protecting the weak?
Lennie has a sweet and not at all malicious desire to spend time with his puppy. He does not realize that handling the puppy can harm it and interfere with its care from its mother and its development of instincts. Despite Lennie's positive intentions, George must protect the puppy from Lennie.

4. "It was obvious that Whit was not interested in his cards. He laid his hand down and George scooped it in. George laid out his deliberate solitaire hand—seven cards and six on top, and five on top of those."

How does the failed euchre game with Whit relate to the theme of companionship/isolation?
Outside of games like solitaire, which George plays multiple times in the bunk house, cards are a social game. The failed card game is a metaphor for the way that men do not connect personally—just as the men find the relationship between George and Lennie somewhat odd.

Of Mice And Men Chapter 3: Elements of Fiction & Literary Devices Suggested Answers Page 2

5. "…Susy's got nice chairs to set in, too. If a guy don't want a flop, why he can just set in the chairs and have a couple or three shots and pass the time of day and Susy don't give a damn. She ain't rushin' guys through and kickin' 'em out if they don't want a flop…."
…
"Me an' Lennie's rollin' up a stake," said George. "I might go in an' set and have a shot, but I ain't puttin' out no two and a half."
…
George sighed. "You give me a good whore house every time," he said. "A guy can go in an' get drunk and get ever'thing outta his system all at once, an' no messes. And he knows how much it's gonna set him back. There here jail baits is just set on the trigger of the hoosegow."

Consider Whit's description of whorehouses and George's response, as well as George's reminder to Lennie about Andy Cushman. What is being suggested by the text about women? George continually states that he is saving his money, as if to say that prostitutes will con men out of their earnings. George says Andy Cushman is in jail as a result of being mixed up with a woman. To George, women seem to represent potential threats to men.

Of Mice And Men Chapter 3
Reading Activity 7: Meaning and Inferences

Anchor Standard	8th Grade	9th-10th Grade
CCRA.R.1	RL.8.1	RL.9-10.1
CCRA.SL.1	SL.8.1	SL.9-10.1

Objective
Students will answer questions about selected passages from the text which require them to extract meaning or inferences from the text.

Directions
The following pages contain passages from Chapter 3 of *Of Mice and Men* and questions related to the passages that require close reading to answer. Students should answer the questions related to the passages.

This can be done as a whole-class activity, individually, or in small groups. If it is done individually or in small groups, come together as a class to discuss the answers to the questions.

Follow-Up/Assessment/Extension
Collect the worksheets for review and/or grading.

Of Mice and Men Chapter 3: Meaning & Inferences 1

Read the passages and answer the related questions.

1. *George said, "She's gonna make a mess. They's gonna be a bad mess about her. She's a jail bait all set on the trigger. That Curley got his work cut out for him. Ranch with a bunch of guys on it ain't no place for a girl, specially like her."*

What does "mess" mean in the passage? Do both uses have the same meaning?

_____
_____
_____
_____

2. *Curley looked threateningly about the room. "Where the hell's Slim?"*
"Went out in the barn," said George. "He was gonna put some tar on a split hoof."
Curley's shoulders dropped and squared. "How long ago'd he go?"

Why is the mention of Curley's shoulders significant?

_____
_____
_____
_____

3. *…We'd have a setter dog and a couple stripe cats, but you gotta watch out them cats don't get the little rabbits."*
Lennie breathed hard. "You jus' let 'em try to get the rabbits. I'll break their God damn necks. I'll . . . . I'll smash 'em with a stick." He subsided, grumbling to himself, threatening the future cats which might dare to disturb the future rabbits.

Does Lennie mean what he says?

_____
_____
_____
_____

Of Mice And Men Chapter 3: Meaning & Inferences 1 Page 2

4. *"You seen what they done to my dog tonight? They says he wasn't no good to himself nor nobody else. When they can me here I wisht somebody'd shoot me. But they won't do nothing like that. I won't have no place to go, an' I can't get no more jobs.*

In what ways is Candy identifying with his dog?

5. *Slim smiled wryly. He knelt down beside Curley. "You got your senses in hand enough to listen?" he asked. Curley nodded. "Well, then listen," Slim went on. "I think you got your han' caught in a machine. If you don't tell nobody what happened, we ain't going to. But you jus' tell an' try to get this guy canned and we'll tell ever'body, an' then will you get the laugh."*

How is the use of the idiom "in hand" ironic here?

Of Mice And Men Chapter 3: Meaning & Inferences 1 Suggested Answers

Read the passages and answer the related questions.

1. George said, "She's gonna make a mess. They's gonna be a bad mess about her. She's a jail bait all set on the trigger. That Curley got his work cut out for him. Ranch with a bunch of guys on it ain't no place for a girl, specially like her."

What does "mess" mean in the passage? Do both uses have the same meaning?
The word is repeated and has slightly different meanings—the first use infers that Curley's wife will be responsible for causing a potentially damaging situation. Since the men have spoken about her in loaded sexualized terms ("tart"), the mess is likely an affair. The second use also suggests a negative situation, but something for which Curley's wife is only indirectly responsible, as if the ripple effect of her "mess" will cause another one that is "bad," conceivably because it will affect a man and potentially ruin his life.

2. Curley looked threateningly about the room. "Where the hell's Slim?"
"Went out in the barn," said George. "He was gonna put some tar on a split hoof."
Curley's shoulders dropped and squared. "How long ago'd he go?"

Why is the mention of Curley's shoulders significant?
Curley's physical movements are those of a boxer—in moments when it is not necessarily appropriate to assume the stance of a boxer, Curley does. His body language speaks volumes about who he is—mostly a bully bent on hurting people to prop up his own stature and manhood.

3. ...We'd have a setter dog and a couple stripe cats, but you gotta watch out them cats don't get the little rabbits."
Lennie breathed hard. "You jus' let 'em try to get the rabbits. I'll break their God damn necks. I'll . . . . I'll smash 'em with a stick." He subsided, grumbling to himself, threatening the future cats which might dare to disturb the future rabbits.

Does Lennie mean what he says?
The reader does not have any reason to doubt Lennie's threats, but the reader also understands that Lennie does not have the intellect to reasonably determine how much force is too much force, so it is threatening. It's not the impulse toward violence so much but the lack of a conceptual frame around it that does foreshadow later events in the novel.

4. "You seen what they done to my dog tonight? They says he wasn't no good to himself nor nobody else. When they can me here I wisht somebody'd shoot me. But they won't do nothing like that. I won't have no place to go, an' I can't get no more jobs.

In what ways is Candy identifying with his dog?
He recognizes that when he is no longer useful, that he is disposable, just as Carlson felt the dog was. In a way, this also foreshadows what happens to Lennie later in the book.

Of Mice And Men Chapter 3: Meaning & Inferences 1 Suggested Answers Page 2

5. *Slim smiled wryly. He knelt down beside Curley. "You got your senses in hand enough to listen?" he asked. Curley nodded. "Well, then listen," Slim went on. "I think you got your han' caught in a machine. If you don't tell nobody what happened, we ain't going to. But you jus' tell an' try to get this guy canned and we'll tell ever'body, an' then will you get the laugh."*

How is the use of the idiom "in hand" ironic here?
"In hand" means to be in control of, and here Curley is very much not in control of the situation. Lennie took control of the physical altercation and Slim took control of its aftermath. Of course, the word "hand" resonates with Curley in multiple ways—his glove of Vaseline and his mangled hand, damaged severely by Lennie.

Of Mice And Men Chapter 3: Meaning & Inferences 2

Read the passage and answer the related questions.

George looked over at Slim and saw the calm, Godlike eyes fastened on him. "Funny," said George. "I used to have a hell of a lot of fun with 'im. Used to play jokes on 'im 'cause he was too dumb to take care of 'imself. But he was too dumb even to know he had a joke played on him. I had fun. Made me seem God damn smart alongside of him. Why he'd do any damn thing I tol' him. If I tol' him to walk over a cliff, over he'd go. That wasn't so damn much fun after a while. He never got mad about it, neither. I've beat the hell outa him, and he coulda bust every bone in my body jus' with his han's, but he never lifted a finger against me." George's voice was taking on the tone of confession. "Tell you what made me stop that. One day a bunch of guys was standin' around up on the Sacramento River. I was feelin' pretty smart. I turns to Lennie and says, 'Jump in.' An' he jumps. Couldn't swim a stroke. He damn near drowned before we could get him. An' he was so damn nice to me for pullin' him out. Clean forgot I told him to jump in. Well, I ain't done nothing like that no more."

1. How has George's treatment of Lennie changed over time?

2. What is George's tone in the passage? What does that suggest about his morality?

3. What words in the passage are synonyms for intelligence? Are they positively or negatively connoted?

Of Mice And Men Chapter 3: Meaning & Inferences 2 Page 2

4. What does George suggest about power and authority in their relationship?

5. What is the effect of Lennie's response to being saved from drowning on George?

Of Mice and Men Chapter 3: Meaning & Inferences 2 Suggested Answers

Read the passage and answer the related questions.

George looked over at Slim and saw the calm, Godlike eyes fastened on him. "Funny," said George. "I used to have a hell of a lot of fun with 'im. Used to play jokes on 'im 'cause he was too dumb to take care of 'imself. But he was too dumb even to know he had a joke played on him. I had fun. Made me seem God damn smart alongside of him. Why he'd do any damn thing I tol' him. If I tol' him to walk over a cliff, over he'd go. That wasn't so damn much fun after a while. He never got mad about it, neither. I've beat the hell outa him, and he coulda bust every bone in my body jus' with his han's, but he never lifted a finger against me." George's voice was taking on the tone of confession. "Tell you what made me stop that. One day a bunch of guys was standin' around up on the Sacramento River. I was feelin' pretty smart. I turns to Lennie and says, 'Jump in.' An' he jumps. Couldn't swim a stroke. He damn near drowned before we could get him. An' he was so damn nice to me for pullin' him out. Clean forgot I told him to jump in. Well, I ain't done nothing like that no more."

1. How has George's treatment of Lennie changed over time?
George used to use Lennie as a form of amusement—he was too trusting and too feeble-minded to recognize when George put him into threatening situations. After a nearly fatal drowning accident, George recognized Lennie's trusting goodness and began to care for him, respect him and protect him. While Lennie may be strong and big, he is actually weak in the sense that he is vulnerable, and George stopped taking advantage of that.

2. What is George's tone in the passage? What does that suggest about his morality?
His tone is "of confession," which suggests that he feels his past behavior has been immoral, almost sinful, and that it is burdensome.

3. What words in the passage are synonyms for intelligence? Are they positively or negatively connoted?
George says "*I was feelin' pretty smart,*" and it is negatively connoted. As he tells the story, he is the villain, and "smart" suggests the opposite of truly intelligent, meaning instead arrogant and superior.

4. What does George suggest about power and authority in their relationship?
That power and authority are not always apparent and that they are not always physical. Lennie is larger and more powerful than George, yet endured severe beatings from George. Lennie never hit or harmed George despite his ability to do so.

5. What is the effect of Lennie's response to being saved from drowning on George?
George recognizes Lennie's child-like attitude and dependence. George becomes Lennie's champion and protector rather than petty harasser.

Of Mice And Men Chapter 3
Writing Activity 1: How Is Weakness Or Strength Determined?

Anchor Standard	8th Grade	9th-10th Grade
CCRA.SL.1	SL.8.1, 1a-1d	SL.9-10.1, 1a-1d
CCRA.SL.3	SL.8.4	SL.9-10.4
CCRA.W.1	W.8.2	W.9-10.2
CCRA.W.2	W.8.4	W.9-10.4
CCRA.W.4	W.8.5	W.9-10.5
CCRA.W.5		W.9-10.7
		W.9-10.9, 9b

Objectives
- Students will evaluate and analyze textual evidence to define the concepts of strength and weakness.
- Students will evaluate passages that reveal characterization, motive and conflict.
- Students will examine language for ways in which characterization, motive and conflict illuminate the definitions of weakness and strength presented in the novel.
- Students will write a composition in which they consider their analysis of relevant passages to answer the question, "How is weakness or strength determined?"

Directions
The following series of worksheets and information organizers can be used by students individually, in small groups, or done partly as a whole-class activity. They are intended to guide students through the process of reading and thinking critically about information by ultimately answering the single question, "How is weakness or strength determined?"

Preview the following pages. Determine the best way to have your particular class handle this assignment (individually, pairs, groups, whole-class, or some combination). A combination of group work (to do the analyzing of the text on the chart page) followed by individual work (to do the second and third pages of the assignment) would most likely be best to fulfill the standards listed for this assignment.

Follow-Up/Assessment/Extension
- The written assignment will be a good basis for assessment of the students' success with this assignment. Create a rubric explaining the criteria on which their written assignments will be evaluated.
- Tell students to continue observing examples of how weakness and strength are depicted in the novel. Consider how these relate to race, gender and social position.
- Have some students read/present their writing assignments to the class to practice more speaking/listening skills and to expose all students to each others' ideas.
- Use this assignment to introduce the themes of strength, weakness and justice.

Of Mice and Men Chapter 3: How Is Weakness Or Strength Determined?

In chapter 3, weakness and strength are concepts interrogated by the physical confrontation that occurs between Curley and Lennie.

In the novel, though, the concepts are presented in a paradoxical way. For example, Lennie, who is physically imposing, has the last name "small." Curley, a former boxer who is constantly looking to tussle with someone, is physically small in stature. This paradoxical presentation calls into question what the qualities of weakness and strength are.

Using textual evidence from Chapter 3, look for patterns to begin formulating an answer to the question "How is weakness or strength determined?". In what ways do Steinbeck's characters subvert expectations about what it usually means to be weak or strong?

To formulate an idea about how weakness or strength is determined:

1. Identify passages and quotes from the scene which describes Lennie and Curley's physical altercation.

2. Examine the context of your quotes.

3. Consider the connotation and denotation of key phrases in your quotes.

    a. What is the tone—is it aggressive, complacent, scared?
    b. Is there a conflict?
    c. How do other characters react, and what do their reactions suggest about strength and weakness?

4. Look for patterns in your evidence. Is a word or idea repeated? Use these patterns to shape an answer to the question.

Of Mice And Men Chapter 3: How Is Weakness Or Strength Determined? Page 2

Complete the chart to analyze information to develop ideas to write your essay.

Incident	Quote/Passage	Observations	What does it express about strength or weakness—physically or morally?
Curley picks fight with Lennie			
Lennie is frightened			
Lennie hurts Curley			

Of Mice And Men Chapter 3: How Is Weakness Or Strength Determined? Page 3

Incident	Quote/Passage	Observations	What does it express about strength or weakness—physically or morally?
Other characters respond			
Lennie tries to make sense of what happened			

Of Mice And Men Chapter 3: How Is Weakness Or Strength Determined? Page 4

A. Evaluate Your Textual Evidence

1. What motivates Curley?

2. Is Lennie's resistance to fighting a sign of weakness or strength?

3. How do other people perceive Curley and Lennie—is one weaker or stronger?

4. How do Curley and Lennie challenge conventional definitions of weakness and strength?

B. Make Notes About Your Conclusions

Of Mice And Men Chapter 3
Suggested Writing Assignments

Anchor Standard	8th Grade	9th-10th Grade
CCRA.W.1	W.8.1, 1a-1d	W.9-10.1, 1a-1e
CCRA.W.2	W.8.2, 2a-2f	W.9-10.2, 2a-2f
CCRA.W.3	W.8.3, 3a-3e	W.9-10.3, 3a-3e
CCRA.W.4	W.8.4	W.9-10.4
CCRA.W.5	W.8.5	W.9-10.5

Objective
Students will be assigned or will choose one of a selection of writing assignments pertaining to Chapter 3 of *Of Mice and Men* to fulfill one or more of the standards listed above.

Directions
To provide you with maximum flexibility for differentiated instruction, the following page has a list of suggested writing assignments, all related to Chapter 3 of *Of Mice and Men*. Either assign individual students particular assignments to do or allow students to choose their own assignments.

A second page of "Quick Write" topics is also included.

Follow-Up/Assessment/Extension
- Have dramatic readings of students' narratives or poems.
- Create a "reading room" space in your classroom where students can donate their writing assignments for others in the class to read.
- Allow students to do more than one assignment if they want to.
- Use the "left-over" assignments (not chosen for this activity) as topics for journal entries.

Of Mice and Men Chapter 3: Creative Analytical Writing Assignments

1. Write the story of Candy's dog, recalling its vitality and youth.

2. Imagine you are George. Why do you like to play solitaire?

3. Write dialogue of what you think Candy should have said when Slim agreed with Carlson over the old dog's fate.

4. Write a narrative description of Candy's shooting of the dog.

5. As Curley was overpowered during his altercation with Lennie, what might Curley have been thinking?

6. Write a flashback scene about the time George's cruelty toward Lennie almost caused Lennie to drown.

7. Write a stream-of-consciousness from Curley's point of view in which he admits why he feels self-conscious and inferior to others.

8. Describe what it might have been like for George and Lennie to hide in the irrigation ditch.

9. Write a flashback scene of George meeting Lennie.

10. Write a letter to the magazine editor expressing how the articles give ranch hands a feeling of hope and community.

Of Mice and Men Chapter 3: Quick-Write Writing Assignments

1. Is Lennie like George's pet in some ways? How?
2. Compare the brothels described. Why is one preferred over the other?
3. Is Carlson right about the dog?
4. What does Candy fear?
5. Why is it significant that George mentions his "stake" so many times?
6. Why does Slim have so much moral authority?
7. Does Curley get what he deserves?
8. Why is Lennie so upset by the physical altercation?
9. Is George's earlier poor treatment of Lennie surprising?
10. What "foreshadows" from earlier chapters have already transpired?

MATERIALS: CHAPTER 4
OF MICE AND MEN

Reading Activity 1: True or False?

Reading Activity 2: Analyzing Passages

Reading Activity 3: Direct vs. Indirect Characterization

Reading Activity 4: Action, Character, Decision

Reading Activity 5: Figurative Language

Reading Activity 6: Elements of Fiction & Literary Devices

Reading Activity 7: Meaning and Inferences

Writing Activity 1: What Are The Effects Of Isolation?

Suggested Writing Assignments

Quick-Write Assignments

NOTES
OF MICE AND MEN

Of Mice And Men Chapter 4
Reading Activity 1: True or False?

Anchor Standard	8th Grade	9th-10th Grade
CCRA.R.1	RL.8.1	RL.9-10.1
CCRA.SL.1	SL.8.1	SL.9-10.1
CCRA.SL.4	SL.8.4	SL.9-10.4

Objectives
- Students will be able to cite the parts of the text that support their analysis of what the text says or infers.
- Students will consider statements about the text, determine whether those statements are true or false, and will give textual evidence supporting their choices.
- Students will work together in small groups to discuss, analyze, and evaluate the statements made.
- Students will evaluate the analytical work of their peers.

Directions
Prior to reading Chapter 4: Give students (or post) the following list of statements about the chapters, and explain to students that they should read Chapter 4 to find out if these statements are true or false:

> Lennie is unaware of racism.
> Crooks suffers from chronic pain from his crooked spine.
> Crooks is protective and caring toward Lennie.
> Crooks dislikes being alone because he cannot ask someone else if they also saw or experienced something unusual.
> Curley's wife had a successful career as a theater actress.
> Curley's wife believes that if she accused Crooks of violence toward her that he would be killed.

After reading Chapter 4: The worksheets on the following pages can be done by students individually, in small groups, or as a whole class. Below are directions to use the questions as a group activity to fulfill more state standards:

- Cut the worksheet apart, making each question and answer box a slip.
- Divide your class into six groups and give one question and a True/False evaluation form to each group. Tell students they are to discuss the statement and determine if the statement is true or false, supporting their decision with evidence from the text. Tell them their answers will be evaluated on the criteria given on the evaluation form.
- Give students ample time to discuss the statements and record their answers.
- Have the groups swap True or False question slips so that each group can evaluate another group's answer. The group should fill in the number of the question they are evaluating, decide how well the answer fulfills the criteria listed, and fill out the form accordingly.
- Repeat the previous step until all the groups have evaluated each others' answers.
- Collect the evaluations and answer slips.

Of Mice And Men Chapter 4 Reading Activity 1: True or False? Lesson Page 2

Follow-Up/Assessment/Extension:

- You could average and record the grades each group received for its answers.
- Students could write in their journals or notebooks one thing they learned from this activity.
- You could hold a whole-class discussion about each or any of the statements, either solely orally or using a blank True or False Worksheet on your whiteboard, filling it in as the discussion unfolds.
- At the beginning of the next class, you could hold a brief discussion reviewing the facts addressed by the True/False Worksheet, to see what students have retained and to reinforce the information.
- You could have students make up (and fill in) their own True/False Worksheets for other information located within this chapter.

Of Mice And Men Chapter 4: True or False?

Write *True* or *False* in the blank next to each statement. Below the statement, explain why you chose true or false, referencing the text to support your choices.

_____ 1. Lennie is unaware of racism.

_____ 2. Crooks suffers from chronic pain from his crooked spine.

_____ 3. Crooks is protective and caring toward Lennie.

Of Mice And Men Chapter 4 True or False? Page 2

_____ 4. Crooks dislikes being alone because he cannot ask someone else if they also saw or experienced something unusual.

_____ 5. Curley's wife had a successful career as a theater actress

_____ 6. Curley's wife believes that if she accused Crooks of violence toward her that he would be killed.

Of Mice And Men Chapter 4 True or False? Evaluation

List Your Group's Members: Your Group's Question # _____

_____   _____   _____

_____   _____   _____

1 = No, Not At All **2** = A Little **3** = Some **4** = Yes **5** = Yes, Very Well

Evaluation of Question # ___
Does the explanation support the answer of true or false?   1 2 3 4 5
Is there good textual evidence to support the answer?   1 2 3 4 5
Is the answer clearly stated?   1 2 3 4 5
                                 Total Score _____ of a possible 15 points

Evaluation of Question # ___
Does the explanation support the answer of true or false?   1 2 3 4 5
Is there good textual evidence to support the answer?   1 2 3 4 5
Is the answer clearly stated?   1 2 3 4 5
                                 Total Score _____ of a possible 15 points

Evaluation of Question # ___
Does the explanation support the answer of true or false?   1 2 3 4 5
Is there good textual evidence to support the answer?   1 2 3 4 5
Is the answer clearly stated?   1 2 3 4 5
                                 Total Score _____ of a possible 15 points

Evaluation of Question # ___
Does the explanation support the answer of true or false?   1 2 3 4 5
Is there good textual evidence to support the answer?   1 2 3 4 5
Is the answer clearly stated?   1 2 3 4 5
                                 Total Score _____ of a possible 15 points

Evaluation of Question # ___
Does the explanation support the answer of true or false?   1 2 3 4 5
Is there good textual evidence to support the answer?   1 2 3 4 5
Is the answer clearly stated?   1 2 3 4 5
                                 Total Score _____ of a possible 15 points

Of Mice And Men Chapter 4: True or False? Suggested Answers

Write *True* or *False* in the blank next to each statement. Below the statement, explain why you chose true or false, referencing the text to support your choices.

<u>TRUE</u> 1. Lennie is unaware of racism.

> Lennie has no idea that he should not be entering Crooks' bunk because a white man would feel too superior to enter it. He recognizes Crooks only as someone to talk to and reiterates this and explains that seeing his light on seemed like an invitation. Lennie is confused by Crooks's vociferous defense of his space and his rights.

<u>TRUE</u> 2. Crooks suffers from chronic pain from his crooked spine.

> He is described as a "cripple." His chronic pain literally shows on his face: "His lean face was lined with deep black wrinkles, and he had thin, pain-tightened lips which were lighter than his face." Throughout the chapter he is seen rubbing liniment on his sore back.

<u>FALSE</u> 3. Crooks is protective and caring toward Lennie.

> Recognizing that Lennie is not conventionally intelligent, Crooks takes liberties with him and suggests that George is going to abandon him. Crooks, himself the target of much prejudice and cruelty, is unkind to Lennie on purpose: "Crooks' face lighted with pleasure in his torture."

<u>TRUE</u> 4. Crooks dislikes being alone because he cannot ask someone else if they also saw or experienced something unusual.

> Crooks describes a particular type of isolation where a person begins to lose a frame of reference for the world he experiences because of isolation from others: "Maybe if he sees somethin', he don't know whether it's right or not. He can't turn to some other guy and ast him if he sees it too. He can't tell. He got nothing to measure by. I seen things out here. I wasn't drunk. I don't know if I was asleep. If some guy was with me, he could tell me I was asleep, an' then it would be all right. But I jus' don't know."

Of Mice And Men Chapter 4 True or False? Suggested Answers Page 2

FALSE 5. Curley's wife had a successful career as a theater actress.

> Just like the ranchers dream of having different lives, Curley's wife is preoccupied with what could have been, a career in the movies: "I tell ya I could of went with shows. Not jus' one, neither. An' a guy tol' me he could put me in pitchers...."

TRUE 6. Curley's wife believes that if she accused Crooks of violence toward her that he would be killed.

> After Crooks shares his intention to ask the boss to disallow Curley's wife to enter the barn, she turns on him venomously: "She turned on him in scorn. "Listen, Nigger," she said. "You know what I can do to you if you open your trap?" Later, she repeats the phrase "You know what I could do?" intimating a threat not just of violence, but death by lynching because even if it is a lie, the word of a white woman against a black man is more highly esteemed and valued by society.

Of Mice And Men Chapter 4
Reading Activity 2: Analyzing Passages

Anchor Standard	8th Grade	9th-10th Grade
CCRA.R.6	RL.8.1	RL.9-10.1
	RL.8.3	
	RL.8.4	RL.9-10.4
	RL.8.6	
CCRA.SL.1	SL.8.1	SL.9-10.1

Objectives
- Students will analyze what the text says explicitly as well as inferences drawn from the text.
- Students will analyze how different points of view of the characters and the audience (or reader) creates suspense or humor.
- Students will analyze the impact of specific word choices on meaning and tone.

Directions
On the pages that follow, there are 8 passages to analyze, each with a question or questions to guide the process. There are many ways to use these questions:

- You could use them as a worksheet for all students to complete individually.
- You could use the worksheet as your guide in a whole-class discussion. Have students turn to the first passage in the book, read it, then ask the question(s) orally. Repeat through all 8 questions.
- You could assign one passage to each of 8 different groups of students, for the students to discuss and come up with responses to the question(s). Then hold a whole-class discussion.
- You could read the passage and then see which student can find the passage first (to practice skimming skills). Then follow up with the questions(s) and discussion.
- You could have students choose one or two questions to respond to in writing in their notebooks or journals.

Follow-Up/Assessment/Extension
- Have students write about Candy's hesitation. What does it suggest about the way people interact on the ranch?
- Have students pick out other passages in this chapter that show interesting word usage, descriptions, or lack of clarity.
- As an introduction to this activity and this chapter, ask students to write about how men represent a potential threat to women and how women represent a potential threat to men. What power does language have as a potential threat?

Of Mice And Men Chapter 4 Analyzing Passages

Answer the questions following the quotations completely.

1. "...You go on get outta my room. I ain't wanted in the bunk house, and you ain't wanted in my room."
 "Why ain't you wanted?" Lennie asked.
 "'Cause I'm black..."

Why is the repetition of "ain't" significant?

2. "George can tell you screwy things, and it don't matter It's just the talking. It's just bein' with another guy. That's all."

Why is talking important to Crooks?

3. ""You're nuts." Crooks was scornful. "I seen hunderds of men come by on the road an' on the ranches, with their bindles on their back an' that same damn thing in their heads. Hunderds of them. They come, an' they quit an' go on; an' every damn one of 'em's got a little piece of land in his head. An' never a God damn one of 'em ever gets it. Just like heaven. Ever'body wants a little piece of lan'. I read plenty of books out here. Nobody never gets to heaven, and nobody gets no land. It's just in their head. They're all the time talkin' about it, but it's jus' in their head."

What is Crooks comparing "heaven" to? Is it attainable?

Of Mice And Men Chapter 4 Analyzing Passages Page 2

4. Candy leaned against the wall beside the broken collar while he scratched his wrist stump. "I been here a long time," he said. "An' Crooks been here a long time. This's the first time I ever been in his room."

What is the significance of the details in the passage, particularly the "broken collar" and "wrist stump"?

5. Well, you keep your place then, Nigger. I could get you strung up on a tree so easy it ain't even funny."

Crooks had reduced himself to nothing. There was no personality, no ego—nothing to arouse either like or dislike. He said, "Yes, ma'am," and his voice was toneless.

In what ways does Crooks change? What prompts this?

6. The stable buck went on dreamily, "I remember when I was little kid on my old man's chicken ranch. Had two brothers. They was always near me, always there. Used to sleep right in the same room, right in the same bed—all three. Had a strawberry patch. Had an alfalfa patch. Used to turn the chickens out in the alfalfa on a sunny morning. My brothers'd set on a fence rail an' watch 'em—white chickens they was."

Compare Crooks' nostalgic memories to his current situation.

Of Mice And Men Chapter 4 Analyzing Passages Page 3

7. Candy said, "That bitch didn't ought to of said that to you."

"It wasn't nothing," Crooks said dully. "You guys comin' in an' settin' made me forget. What she says is true."

Do Candy and Crooks share the same outlook on Curley's wife?

8. "Awright," she said contemptuously. "Awright, cover 'im up if ya wanta. Whatta I care? You bindle bums think you're so damn good. Whatta ya think I am, a kid? I tell ya I could of went with shows. Not jus' one, neither. An' a guy tol' me he could put me in pitchers…" She was breathless with indignation. "—Sat'iday night. Ever'body out doin' som'pin'. Ever'body! An' what am I doin'? Standin' here talkin' to a bunch of bindle stiffs—a nigger an' a dum-dum and a lousy ol' sheep—an' likin' it because they ain't nobody else."

What is causing Curley's wife's "indignation" and anger?

Of Mice And Men Chapter 4 Analyzing Passages Suggested Answers

Answer the questions following the quotations completely.

1. "...You go on get outta my room. I ain't wanted in the bunk house, and you ain't wanted in my room."
 "Why ain't you wanted?" Lennie asked.
 "'Cause I'm black..."

Why is the repetition of "ain't" significant?
The repetition is a way to convey Crooks's sense of "fairness" over access to his living quarters and his being denied access to the men's bunk house. Crooks maintains that it is his "right" to deny access to Lennie (and others); this give him a sense of authority, even if it is in actuality false. The "ain't"—applied to both Crooks and Lennie—shows that sense of "equality."

2. "George can tell you screwy things, and it don't matter It's just the talking. It's just bein' with another guy. That's all."

Why is talking important to Crooks?
Crooks begins to see the value of a companion like Lennie, and as he talks to him, his "excitement increase[s]." Crooks realizes that it does not even matter what he says to Lennie ("screwy things"), but it is the "just bein' with another guy." As Crooks continues, he explains that if he had a companion, he could ask him to verify if the things he sees and experiences are real. So, to Crooks, conversation seems to provide a validation of who he is.

3. ""You're nuts." Crooks was scornful. "I seen hunderds of men come by on the road an' on the ranches, with their bindles on their back an' that same damn thing in their heads. Hunderds of them. They come, an' they quit an' go on; an' every damn one of 'em's got a little piece of land in his head. An' never a God damn one of 'em ever gets it. Just like heaven. Ever'body wants a little piece of lan'. I read plenty of books out here. Nobody never gets to heaven, and nobody gets no land. It's just in their head. They're all the time talkin' about it, but it's jus' in their head."

What is Crooks comparing "heaven" to? Is it attainable?
Crooks compares owning land to heaven. What is interesting is that Crooks suggests that it is not attainable, that it is like some mythology, something that can be believed in but never proven as a real possibility or actual outcome. When people die, they cannot prove to people who are alive that heaven exists—that same lack of proof of land ownership is what Crooks describes.

4. Candy leaned against the wall beside the broken collar while he scratched his wrist stump. "I been here a long time," he said. "An' Crooks been here a long time. This's the first time I ever been in his room."

What is the significance of the details in the passage, particularly the "broken collar" and "wrist stump"?
There is a connection between Candy, Crooks, and Candy's dog—all have a physical disability. Crooks's job is to care for the animals and to repair things—he is a fixer. Like the collar, Candy himself is broken. They are all left behind and are the weakest of the men.

Of Mice And Men Chapter 4 Analyzing Passages Suggested Answers Page 2

5. Well, you keep your place then, Nigger. I could get you strung up on a tree so easy it ain't even funny."

Crooks had reduced himself to nothing. There was no personality, no ego—nothing to arouse either like or dislike. He said, "Yes, ma'am," and his voice was toneless.

In what ways does Crooks change? What prompts this?
After expressing his opinion to Curley's wife about her behavior, Crooks is quickly reminded by her of his place in the social order on the ranch, and as a black man, it is at the bottom. By expressing his opinion, he expressed his individuality, which was unrecognized by and not tolerated by society at the time. It is noteworthy that she addresses him with the epithet "Nigger," as a way to strip him of individuality, and as a consequence, he becomes "reduced," "nothing," "no personality," "no ego," and "toneless." The threat she makes about a violent death is serious because it is real.

6. The stable buck went on dreamily, "I remember when I was little kid on my old man's chicken ranch. Had two brothers. They was always near me, always there. Used to sleep right in the same room, right in the same bed—all three. Had a strawberry patch. Had an alfalfa patch. Used to turn the chickens out in the alfalfa on a sunny morning. My brothers'd set on a fence rail an' watch 'em—white chickens they was."

Compare Crooks' nostalgic memories to his current situation.
His nostalgia reveals his deep longing for connection with other people. The way he talks about the physical proximity of his brothers suggests a closeness that he valued and is completely absent in his current situation.

7. Candy said, "That bitch didn't ought to of said that to you."
"It wasn't nothing," Crooks said dully. "You guys comin' in an' settin' made me forget. What she says is true."

Do Candy and Crooks share the same outlook on Curley's wife?
They don't, and the difference is race. Candy cannot understand the gravity of the threat toward Crooks and how Crooks is effectively stripped of any agency or individuality or opinion that he might have. He understands that as a black man, he is subject to the whims of a white woman, even if they are false, and he knows that to unfortunately be "true."

8. "Awright," she said contemptuously. "Awright, cover 'im up if ya wanta. Whatta I care? You bindle bums think you're so damn good. Whatta ya think I am, a kid? I tell ya I could of went with shows. Not jus' one, neither. An' a guy tol' me he could put me in pitchers..." She was breathless with indignation. "—Sat'iday night. Ever'body out doin' som'pin'. Ever'body! An' what am I doin'? Standin' here talkin' to a bunch of bindle stiffs—a nigger an' a dum-dum and a lousy ol' sheep—an' likin' it because they ain't nobody else."

What is causing Curley's wife's "indignation" and anger?
She feels put down and denigrated by others and perceives that others feel superior to her (even if that is not true and is just her perception). She is left out, and it is particularly difficult for her because she is someone who likes to be the center of attention (i.e. wanting to be a movie actress). Her anger is also rooted in how she had a dream but it did not come true, but ended up with a difficult alternative, being married to Curley and facing extreme isolation.

Of Mice And Men Chapter 4
Reading Activity 3: Direct vs. Indirect Characterization

Anchor Standard	8th Grade	9th-10th Grade
CCRA.R.1	RL.8.1	RL.9-10.1
CCRA.SL.1	SL.8.1	SL.9-10.1

Objective
Using textual evidence, students will explore the subtleties of character development.

Directions
The direct vs. indirect characterization worksheet on the following page could be used in many ways, completed by small groups of students, individual students, or as a whole class activity.

Students can use their current observations about the characters to understand ways that important information about characters is conveyed directly or indirectly.

Students may (and should) use their books to skim through the chapter to refresh their memories or gather more information about the characters.

After students complete the worksheets discuss students' answers as a whole class. Collect the worksheets for grading, if you choose, or have students put them in their notebooks for further study.

Follow-Up/Assessment/Extension
Ask students to consider how characteristics which are fixed (such as race, gender, physical disability and mental disability) define characters. Are these more dominant in determining characterization than other qualities? Why?

Of Mice And Men Chapter 4
Reading Activity 3: Direct vs. Indirect Characterization

Characterization, or the development of characters in a work of fiction, can be direct or indirect. Direct characterization is revealing aspects of character directly to the reader via a narrator, the character him or herself or from another character. Indirect characterization requires readers to infer what a character is like through the character's thoughts, action, diction, appearance and interactions with others.

Complete the chart, using actual quotes when asked and noting page numbers.

Character	Direct Characterization Quote	Indirect Characterization Quote	Indirect Characterization Inference
Crooks			
Lennie			
Candy			
Curley's wife			

Of Mice And Men Chapter 4
Reading Activity 3: Direct vs. Indirect Characterization Suggested Answers

Characterization, or the development of characters in a work of fiction, can be direct or indirect. Direct characterization is revealing aspects of character directly to the reader via a narrator, the character him or herself or from another character. Indirect characterization requires readers to infer what a character is like through the character's thoughts, action, diction, appearance and interactions with others.

Complete the chart, using actual quotes when asked and noting page numbers.

Character	Direct Characterization Quote	Indirect Characterization Quote	Indirect Characterization Inference
Crooks	ANSWERS MAY VARY "S'pose you had to sit out here an' read books. Sure you could play horseshoes till it got dark, but then you got to read books. Books ain't no good. A guy needs somebody to be near him."	Crooks avoided the whole subject now.	Crooks longs to be with the others on the ranch, but knows that as the only black man, he cannot be friends with them because of racism.
Lennie	"Lennie's a nice fella."	Gradually Lennie's interest came around to what was being said.	Lennie is positive and optimistic, but he has not ability to retain an awareness of things that he should be cautious about.
Candy	Candy was crestfallen. "Didn't tell nobody but Crooks."	Old Candy was watching her, fascinated.	Candy is a poor judge of people because he himself is so kind and benevolent.
Curley's wife	"I'm glad you bust up Curley a little bit. He got it comin' to him. Sometimes I'd like to bust him myself."	She looked from one face to another, and they were all closed against her.	She is desperate and deeply unhappy.

Of Mice and Men Chapter 4
Reading Activity 4: Action, Character, Decision

Anchor Standard	8th Grade	9th-10th Grade
CCRA.R.1	RL.8.3	
CCRA.SL.1	SL.8.1	SL.9-10.1

Objective
Students will identify whether particular lines of dialogue or incidents in the story propel the action, reveal aspects of a character, or provoke a decision.

Directions
The following page contains passages from Chapter 4 of Of Mice and Men. Students should determine whether the passages advance the action, reveal aspects of a character, or provoke a decision.
This can be done as a whole-class activity, individually, or in small groups.

Follow-Up/Assessment/Extension
Have students skim Chapter 4 to find one example of a passage that propels the action, one that reveals aspects of a character, and one that provokes a decision. Again, this could be done individually or as a group.

Of Mice and Men Chapter 4: Action, Character, Decision

Write **A** (for Action) **C** (for Character) or **D** (for Decision) in the blank next to each to identify whether the passage/statement advances the action, tells us more about a character, or provokes a decision. On the lines under each question, provide a short explanation of your choice.

___ 1. Crooks possessed several pairs of shoes, a pair of rubber boots, a big alarm clock and a single-barreled shotgun. And he had books, too; a tattered dictionary and a mauled copy of the California civil code for 1905. There were battered magazines and a few dirty books on a special shelf over his bunk. A pair of large gold-rimmed spectacles hung from a nail on the wall above his bed.

___ 2. Crooks scowled, but Lennie's disarming smile defeated him. "Come on in and set a while," Crooks said. "'Long as you won't get out and leave me alone, you might as well set down."

___ 3. "I said s'pose George went into town tonight and you never heard of him no more." Crooks pressed forward some kind of private victory. "Just s'pose that," he repeated.

___ 4. Candy's face had grown redder and redder, but before she was done speaking, he had control of himself. He was the master of the situation. "I might of knew," he said gently. "Maybe you just better go along an' roll your hoop. We ain't got nothing to say to you at all. We know what we got, and we don't care whether you know it or not. So maybe you better jus' scatter along now, 'cause Curley maybe ain't gonna like his wife out in the barn with us 'bindle stiffs.'"

___ 5. "Well, jus' forget it," said Crooks. "I didn't mean it. Jus' foolin'. I wouldn' want to go no place like that."

Of Mice and Men Chapter 4:
Action, Character, Decision Suggested Answers

Write **A** (for Action) **C** (for Character) or **D** (for Decision) in the blank next to each to identify whether the passage/statement advances the action, tells us more about a character, or provokes a decision. On the lines under each question, provide a short explanation of your choice.

C 1. Crooks possessed several pairs of shoes, a pair of rubber boots, a big alarm clock and a single-barreled shotgun. And he had books,too; a tattered dictionary and a mauled copy of the California civil code for 1905. There were battered magazines and a few dirty books on a special shelf over his bunk. A pair of large gold-rimmed spectacles hung from a nail on the wall above his bed.
Crooks's possessions reveal more about who he is and his lifestyle. He has more possessions than most of the ranch hands, and the number of them suggests that he has a job that is much more permanent. The alarm clock is necessary because he is alone—unlike the bunk house, which would have others waking up to get to work on time. His books, dictionary and glasses are all part of his solitary practice of reading.

D 2. Crooks scowled, but Lennie's disarming smile defeated him. "Come on in and set a while," Crooks said. "'Long as you won't get out and leave me alone, you might as well set down."
Despite Crooks's desire to defend his territory (the same to which his skin color relegates him) from Lennie's interloping, the desire for companionship is greater than his sense of indignation.

A 3. "I said s'pose George went into town tonight and you never heard of him no more." Crooks pressed forward some kind of private victory. "Just s'pose that," he repeated.
Crooks is recognizing that he can take liberties with Lennie because he is not so smart and is cruel, suggesting that George might abandon him. This moves the action forward because Lennie is pushed to the point when the scariness and unpredictability of his anger shows.

A 4. Candy's face had grown redder and redder, but before she was done speaking, he had control of himself. He was the master of the situation. "I might of knew," he said gently. "Maybe you just better go along an' roll your hoop. We ain't got nothing to say to you at all. We know what we got, and we don't care whether you know it or not. So maybe you better jus' scatter along now, 'cause Curley maybe ain't gonna like his wife out in the barn with us 'bindle stiffs.'"
Candy creates conflict by standing up to Curley's wife and denying her the attention she is starving for ("We ain't got nothing to say…"). The conflict sets up and foreshadows later major events in the novel.

D 5. "Well, jus' forget it," said Crooks. "I didn't mean it. Jus' foolin'. I wouldn' want to go no place like that."
After the jarring encounter with Curley's wife (and her real threat of violence), Crooks makes a decision to opt out of being part of the farm. The encounter makes Crooks decide that because of race, achieving the dream is an impossibility for him.

Of Mice and Men Chapter 4
Reading Activity 5: Figurative Language

Anchor Standard	8th Grade	9th-10th Grade
CCRA.R.4	RL.8.4	RL.9-10.4
CCRA.SL.1	SL.8.1	SL.9-10.1

Objectives
- Students will determine the meaning of words and phrases as they are used in the text, including figurative and connotative meanings.
- Students will determine how figurative language contributes to meaning, particularly through euphemism.

Directions
The following page has a passage from the text which includes examples of figurative language. This work-sheet can be done individually, as a whole-class activity, or in small groups. Discuss the answers as a whole class. Collect the worksheets and record the grades if you choose to do so.

Follow-Up/Assessment/Extension
Ask students to begin tracking instances of a particular type of figurative language (personification, metaphor, hyperbole, etc.) in the text. Ask students to make a list to track their observations. Assign students a paper that uses these examples to make an argument about how the language creates meaning.

Of Mice And Men Chapter 4: Figurative Language

Read the following passages, and determine if the language is figurative (F) or literal (L). On the lines below, explain any use of figurative language and the effect it has on meaning.

_____1. "You're nuts," said Crooks. "You're crazy as a wedge. What rabbits you talkin' about?"

_____2. "George can tell you screwy things, and it don't matter. It's just the talking. It's just bein' with another guy. That's all."

_____3. Crooks bored in on him. "Want me ta tell ya what'll happen? They'll take ya to the booby hatch. They'll tie ya up with a collar, like a dog."

_____4. "A guy goes nuts if he ain't got nobody."

_____5. "I seen guys nearly crazy with loneliness for land, but ever' time a whore house or a blackjack game took what it takes."

Of Mice And Men Chapter 4: Figurative Language Suggested Answers

Read the following passages, and determine if the language is figurative (F) or literal (L). On the lines below, explain any use of figurative language and the effect it has on meaning.

F 1. "You're nuts," said Crooks. "You're crazy as a wedge. What rabbits you talkin' about?"
Crooks compares Lennie to a "wedge," and while it is accusatory, it has a joking tone.

L 2. "George can tell you screwy things, and it don't matter. It's just the talking. It's just bein' with another guy. That's all."
Here Crooks is being honest and straightforward.

F 3. Crooks bored in on him. "Want me ta tell ya what'll happen? They'll take ya to the booby hatch. They'll tie ya up with a collar, like a dog."
Crooks is deliberately being cruel. He hyperbolizes purposefully to upset Lennie.

F 4. "A guy goes nuts if he ain't got nobody."
Conceivably Crooks is in this state, but he does not seem "nuts," so it is a bit of an exaggeration, created by his use of an idiom.

F 5. "I seen guys nearly crazy with loneliness for land, but ever' time a whore house or a blackjack game took what it takes."
The "whore house" and "blackjack game" are almost personified here, "taking" the money and stake required to buy a farm and achieve a dream.

Of Mice And Men Chapter 4
Reading Activity 6: Elements of Fiction & Literary Devices

Anchor Standard	8th Grade	9th-10th Grade
CCRA.R.1	RL.8.1	RL.9-10.1
	RL.8.2	RL.9-10.2
	RL.8.3	RL.9-10.4
	RL.8.4	RL.9-10.5
	RL.8.6	
CCRA.SL.1	SL.8.1	SL.9-10.1

Objective
Students will study and discuss passages from the text to examine symbol, motif and theme and explore how these create meaning in the text.

Directions
Use the following discussion questions as a guide to discussing symbol, motif and theme, in these chapters. You can give students the questions ahead of time and have them formulate answers prior to the class discussion or you can jump right in with a whole class discussion without student preparation if your students will handle that well.

As you hold the class discussion, be sure to include conversations defining symbol, motif and theme and explaining how these work together to advance meaning in the text.

Follow-Up/Assessment/Extension
After your discussion, ask students to look for recurrences of these symbols, motifs and themes in future chapters.

Of Mice And Men Chapter 4: Elements of Fiction & Literary Devices

One of the primary themes in the novel is fear. Consider the following passages and how Steinbeck presents and defines the concept of fear.

1. Crooks saw the danger as it approached him. He edged back on his bunk to get out of the way. "I was just supposin'," he said. "George ain't hurt. He's all right. He'll be back all right."

What is Crooks afraid of here? How has presenting a hypothetical situation put him in danger?

2. ...Maybe if he sees somethin', he don't know whether it's right or not. He can't turn to some other guy and ast him if he sees it too. He can't tell. He got nothing to measure by. I seen things out here. I wasn't drunk. I don't know if I was asleep. If some guy was with me, he could tell me I was asleep, an' then it would be all right. But I jus' don't know." Crooks was looking across the room now, looking toward the window.

What is Crooks afraid of in this passage? What is the relationship between talking and fear, according to Crooks?

3. "She regarded them amusedly. "Funny thing," she said. "If I catch any one man, and he's alone, I get along fine with him. But just let two of the guys get together an' you won't talk. Jus' nothing but mad." She dropped her fingers and put her hands on her hips. "You're all scared of each other, that's what. Ever' one of you's scared the rest is goin' to get something on you."

What is Curley's wife suggesting that the men on the ranch are afraid of?

Of Mice And Men Chapter 4: Elements of Fiction & Literary Devices Page 2

4. Maybe there was a time when we was scared of gettin' canned, but we ain't no more. We got our own lan', and it's ours, an' we c'n go to it."

What, according to Candy, has allayed the men's fear of being fired?

5. Crooks seemed to come slowly out of the layers of protection he had put on.

What are the "layers of protection," and why has Crooks protected himself?

6. "'Member what I said about hoein' and doin' odd jobs?"
"Yeah," said Candy. "I remember."
"Well, jus' forget it," said Crooks. "I didn't mean it. Jus' foolin'. I wouldn' want to go no place like that."

How does Crooks's changing his mind relate to fear?

Of Mice And Men Chapter 4:
Elements of Fiction & Literary Devices Suggested Answers

One of the primary themes in the novel is fear. Consider the following passages and how Steinbeck presents and defines the concept of fear.

1. Crooks saw the danger as it approached him. He edged back on his bunk to get out of the way. "I was just supposin'," he said. "George ain't hurt. He's all right. He'll be back all right."

What is Crooks afraid of here? How has presenting a hypothetical situation put him in danger?
After deliberately taunting Lennie and suggesting that George might abandon him, Crooks sees how Lennie is not able to modulate his feelings or strength. The thought of George being threatened provokes Lennie, who directs his fear and frustration toward Crooks. Lennie is not able to understand the concept of a hypothetical situation—this shows why Lennie appears to have poor judgment (i.e. the situation in Weed) and why he cannot see the link between cause and effect.

2. ...Maybe if he sees somethin', he don't know whether it's right or not. He can't turn to some other guy and ast him if he sees it too. He can't tell. He got nothing to measure by. I seen things out here. I wasn't drunk. I don't know if I was asleep. If some guy was with me, he could tell me I was asleep, an' then it would be all right. But I jus' don't know." Crooks was looking across the room now, looking toward the window.

What is Crooks afraid of in this passage? What is the relationship between talking and fear, according to Crooks?
Crooks is afraid of literally seeing things that are not there, which he suggests is a function of extreme isolation. Without someone to compare this observations with, he assumes that he might be crazy. Talking helps relive the fear associated with the dissociation from others that happens as a result of isolation.

3. "She regarded them amusedly. "Funny thing," she said. "If I catch any one man, and he's alone, I get along fine with him. But just let two of the guys get together an' you won't talk. Jus' nothing but mad." She dropped her fingers and put her hands on her hips. "You're all scared of each other, that's what. Ever' one of you's scared the rest is goin' to get something on you."

What is Curley's wife suggesting that the men on the ranch are afraid of?
Linked to the theme of isolation, she suggests that any connections, interactions or transactions between men are a source of anxiety and fear for them. The idea of someone else having authority and exercising that authority is scary, as is the idea of being judged by others.

4. Maybe there was a time when we was scared of gettin' canned, but we ain't no more. We got our own lan', and it's ours, an' we c'n go to it."

What, according to Candy, has allayed the men's fear of being fired?
The belief in the dream of the farm is what emboldens Candy. His deepest fear was being displaced from the ranch and having nothing and no one. Now, the farm is a real possibility, and he does not feel dependent on the ranch owners.

Of Mice And Men Chapter 4: Elements of Fiction & Literary Devices Suggested Answers Page 2

5. Crooks seemed to come slowly out of the layers of protection he had put on.

What are the "layers of protection," and why has Crooks protected himself?
After Curley's wife threatens Crooks multiple times about her ability to accuse him of harm so he would be lynched, Crooks retreats from the conversation. The "layers of protection" include looking away from her and addressing her as "maam," as ways to show supplication.

6. "'Member what I said about hoein' and doin' odd jobs?"
"Yeah," said Candy. "I remember."
"Well, jus' forget it," said Crooks. "I didn't mean it. Jus' foolin'. I wouldn' want to go no place like that."

How does Crooks's changing his mind relate to fear?
The word "forget" is used several times in the chapter, particularly when Candy and Lennie's presence in Crooks's room make Crooks "forget" about the way he is treated by society because of his race. Here, Crooks is reminded that unjust, unfair, arbitrary claims from a white woman can literally end his life, and he is scared back into submission, that is, abiding by the unspoken rules that make him powerless in society.

Of Mice And Men Chapter 4
Reading Activity 7: Meaning and Inferences

Anchor Standard	8th Grade	9th-10th Grade
CCRA.R.1	RL.8.1	RL.9-10.1
CCRA.SL.1	SL.8.1	SL.9-10.1

Objective
Students will answer questions about selected passages from the text which require them to extract meaning or inferences from the text.

Directions
The following pages contain passages from Chapter 4 of *Of Mice and Men* and questions related to the passages that require close reading to answer. Students should answer the questions related to the passages.

This can be done as a whole-class activity, individually, or in small groups. If it is done individually or in small groups, come together as a class to discuss the answers to the questions.

Follow-Up/Assessment/Extension
Collect the worksheets for review and/or grading.

Of Mice And Men Chapter 4: Meaning & Inferences 1

Read the passages and answer the related questions.

1. *"I was born right here in California. My old man had a chicken ranch, 'bout ten acres. The white kids come to play at our place, an' sometimes I went to play with them, and some of them was pretty nice. My ol' man didn't like that. I never knew till long later why he didn't like that. But I know now."* He hesitated, and when he spoke again his voice was softer. *"There wasn't another colored family for miles around. And now there ain't a colored man on this ranch an' there's jus' one family in Soledad."*

What didn't Crooks's father like? What did Crooks later understand?

2. *"The stable buck went on dreamily, "I remember when I was a little kid on my old man's chicken ranch. Had two brothers. They was always near me, always there. Used to sleep right in the same room, right in the same bed- all three. Had a strawberry patch. Had an alfalfa patch. Used to turn the chickens out in the alfalfa on a sunny morning. My brothers'd set on a fence rail an' watch 'em- white chickens they was."*

Why is "dreamily" significant? How do Crooks's memories compare to Lennie's dreams for the future?

3. *"Candy came in, but he was still embarrassed, "You got a nice cozy little place in here," he said to Crooks. "Must be nice to have a room all to yourself this way."
"Sure," said Crooks. "And a manure pile under the window. Sure, it's swell."*

Is Crooks's retort justified? Why or why not?

4. *Crooks reached around and explored his spine with his hand. "I never seen a guy really do it," he said. "I seen guys nearly crazy with loneliness for land, but ever' time a whore house or a blackjack game took what it takes." He hesitated. "...If you... guys would want a hand to work for nothing- just his keep, why I'd come an' lend a hand.*

Consider the context of the passage. What changes Crooks's mind, and how is the word "loneliness" significant in that change?

5. *"She stood still in the doorway, smiling a little at them, rubbing the nails of one hand with the thumb and forefinger of the other. And her eyes traveled from one face to another. "They left all the weak ones here," she said finally. "Think I don't know where they all went? Even Curley. I know where they all went."*

What does she mean by "weak ones"?

Of Mice And Men Chapter 4: Meaning & Inferences 1 Suggested Answers

Read the passages and answer the related questions.

1. *"I was born right here in California. My old man had a chicken ranch, 'bout ten acres. The white kids come to play at our place, an' sometimes I went to play with them, and some of them was pretty nice. My ol' man didn't like that. I never knew till long later why he didn't like that. But I know now."* He hesitated, and when he spoke again his voice was softer. *"There wasn't another colored family for miles around. And now there ain't a colored man on this ranch an' there's jus' one family in Soledad."*

What didn't Crooks's father like? What did Crooks later understand?
Crooks's father did not like when he would play with white children. In the context of their ranch, the children may have been equals, and no racism existed. Crooks's father knew—and Crooks eventually learned—that the societal view of race would always apply to his son, no matter where he was. So, despite Crooks being in a similar position as an adult (the only black man around), he will be rejected by white people, and therefore, alone.

2. *"The stable buck went on dreamily, "I remember when I was a little kid on my old man's chicken ranch. Had two brothers. They was always near me, always there. Used to sleep right in the same room, right in the same bed- all three. Had a strawberry patch. Had an alfalfa patch. Used to turn the chickens out in the alfalfa on a sunny morning. My brothers'd set on a fence rail an' watch 'em- white chickens they was."*

Why is "dreamily" significant? How do Crooks's memories compare to Lennie's dreams for the future?
"Dreamily" has two connotations—one that it is pleasant and optimal and the other is that it is unlikely to happen. Basically Crooks is describing Lennie's dream of "living offa the fat o' the land" as he describes his childhood—both are agricultural, pastoral and include constant companionship.

3. *"Candy came in, but he was still embarrassed, "You got a nice cozy little place in here," he said to Crooks."Must be nice to have a room all to yourself this way."*
"Sure," said Crooks. "And a manure pile under the window. Sure, it's swell."

Is Crooks's retort justified? Why or why not?
Candy attempts to offer a compliment, but it is also loaded with other meanings. Candy's comment can be inferred to mean that the place is too nice for Crooks and that the place is nicer than the bunk houses where the white ranchers live. Crooks does not take it as a compliment; he reminds Candy that the accommodations are not preferable to the men's bunk houses because of the isolation and because they are literally next to a pile of manure.

4. *Crooks reached around and explored his spine with his hand. "I never seen a guy really do it," he said. "I seen guys nearly crazy with loneliness for land, but ever' time a whore house or a blackjack game took what it takes." He hesitated. "...If you... guys would want a hand to work for nothing- just his keep, why I'd come an'lend a hand.*

Consider the context of the passage. What changes Crooks's mind, and how is the word "loneliness" significant in that change?

Of Mice And Men Chapter 4: Meaning & Inferences 1 Suggested Answers Page 2

As Crooks is talking, Steinbeck depicts him as in physical pain ("explored his spine") as well as in incredible emotional pain caused by his isolation from others. To use the word "lonely" to describe land is unusual—since land is not necessarily social. But, for Lennie and Candy, land is a decidedly social experience, and Crooks recognizes his own hunger for that.

5. *"She stood still in the doorway, smiling a little at them, rubbing the nails of one hand with the thumb and forefinger of the other. And her eyes traveled from one face to another. "They left all the weak ones here," she said finally. "Think I don't know where they all went? Even Curley. I know where they all went."*

What does she mean by "weak ones"?
She is saying it derisively and cruelly, but these three characters (as well as Curley's wife) are defined by physical traits beyond their control. For Lennie, it is his awesome strength (actually a liability) and slow mind; for Crooks, it is his crooked back, and for Candy it is the loss of his hand. Curley's wife is similarly weak because of a physical attribute: being female.

Of Mice And Men Chapter 4: Meaning & Inferences 2

Read the passage and answer the related questions.

The girl flared up. "Sure I gotta husban'. You all seen him. Swell guy, ain't he? Spends all his time sayin' what he's gonna do to guys he don't like, and he don't like nobody. Think I'm gonna stay in that two-by-four house and listen how Curley's gonna lead with his left twice, and then bring in the ol' right cross? 'One-two,' he says. 'Jus' the ol' one-two an' he'll go down.'" She paused and her face lost its sullenness and grew interested. "Say- what happened to Curley's han'?"

There was an embarrassed silence. Candy stole a look at Lennie. Then he coughed. "Why... Curley... he got his han' caught in a machine, ma'am. Bust his han'."

She watched for a moment, and then she laughed. "Baloney! What you think you're sellin' me? Curley started som'pin' he didn' finish. Caught in a machine- baloney! Why, he ain't give nobody the good ol' one-two since he got his han' bust. Who bust him?"

Candy repeated sullenly, "Got it caught in a machine."

"Awright," she said contemptuously. "Awright, cover 'im up if ya wanta. Whatta I care? You bindle bums think you're so damn good. Whatta ya think I am, a kid? I tell ya I could of went with shows. Not jus' one, neither. An' a guy tol' me he could put me in pitchers...." She was breathless with indignation. "-Sat'iday night. Ever'body out doin' som'pin'. Ever'body! An' what am I doin'? Standin' here talkin' to a bunch of bindle stiffs- a nigger an' a dum-dum and a lousy ol' sheep- an' likin' it because they ain't nobody else."

1. What is Curley's wife's main criticism of her husband?

2. Why is it significant that Curley's wife and Candy are both described as "sullen"?

3. In what ways does Curley's wife suggest that she is considered as less than?

4. Why does Curley's wife insult the men?

5. What is Curley's wife really indignant about?

Of Mice And Men Chapter 4: Meaning & Inferences 2 Suggested Answers

Read the passage and answer the related questions.

The girl flared up. "Sure I gotta husban'. You all seen him. Swell guy, ain't he? Spends all his time sayin' what he's gonna do to guys he don't like, and he don't like nobody. Think I'm gonna stay in that two-by-four house and listen how Curley's gonna lead with his left twice, and then bring in the ol' right cross? 'One-two,' he says. 'Jus' the ol' one-two an' he'll go down.'" She paused and her face lost its sullenness and grew interested. "Say- what happened to Curley's han'?"

There was an embarrassed silence. Candy stole a look at Lennie. Then he coughed. "Why... Curley... he got his han' caught in a machine, ma'am. Bust his han'."

She watched for a moment, and then she laughed. "Baloney! What you think you're sellin' me? Curley started som'pin' he didn' finish. Caught in a machine- baloney! Why, he ain't give nobody the good ol' one-two since he got his han' bust. Who bust him?"

Candy repeated sullenly, "Got it caught in a machine."

"Awright," she said contemptuously. "Awright, cover 'im up if ya wanta. Whatta I care? You bindle bums think you're so damn good. Whatta ya think I am, a kid? I tell ya I could of went with shows. Not jus' one, neither. An' a guy tol' me he could put me in pitchers...." She was breathless with indignation. "-Sat'iday night. Ever'body out doin' som'pin'. Ever'body! An' what am I doin'? Standin' here talkin' to a bunch of bindle stiffs- a nigger an' a dum-dum and a lousy ol' sheep- an' likin' it because they ain't nobody else."

1. What is Curley's wife's main criticism of her husband?
Her main criticism is his belligerent attitude towards other men and his preoccupation for demonstrating his masculinity through might.

2. Why is it significant that Curley's wife and Candy are both described as "sullen"?
The word unites the two of them to be of like mind or emotions. Both uses refer to the characters in their relationships to Curley.

3. In what way does Curley's wife suggest that she is considered as less than others?
She suggests that she is treated in a childish way ("Whattya think I am, a kid?). This is another way people express prejudice; age is an attribute that cannot be changed, yet it is used as the basis to form judgments about people.

4. Why does Curley's wife insult the men?
She calls them insulting names that all have prejudicial beliefs inherent in them: "bindle stiffs (a class designation), "a nigger" (race), "a dum-dum" (disability) and a lousy ol' sheep (age/infirmity). She insults them as a way to make herself feel better, as she, too, is the target of very similar insults ("tart," "bitch").

5. What is Curley's wife really indignant about?
She is angry that she is not respected by Curley and that he does not attempt to know her or create a rapport with her.

Of Mice and Men Chapter 4
Writing Activity 1: What Are The Effects Of Isolation?

Anchor Standard	8th Grade	9th-10th Grade
CCRA.SL.1	SL.8.1, 1a-1d	SL.9-10.1, 1a-1d
CCRA.SL.3	SL.8.4	SL.9-10.4
CCRA.W.1	W.8.2	W.9-10.2
CCRA.W.2	W.8.4	W.9-10.4
CCRA.W.4	W.8.5	W.9-10.5
CCRA.W.5		W.9-10.7
		W.9-10.9, 9b

Objectives
- Students will evaluate and analyze textual evidence to define the concepts of isolation and loneliness within the parameters of the novel.
- Students will evaluate passages that reveal characterization, motive and conflict.
- Students will examine language for ways in which characterization, motive and conflict illuminate the main theme of isolation and loneliness in the novel.
- Students will write a composition in which they consider their analysis of relevant passages to answer the question, "What are the effects of isolation?"

Directions
The following series of worksheets and information organizers can be used by students individually, in small groups, or done partly as a whole-class activity. They are intended to guide students through the process of reading and thinking critically about information by ultimately answering the single question, "What are the effects of isolation?"

Preview the following pages. Determine the best way to have your particular class handle this assignment (individually, pairs, groups, whole-class, or some combination). A combination of group work (to do the analyzing of the text on the chart page) followed by individual work (to do the second and third pages of the as-assignment) would most likely be best to fulfill the standards listed for this assignment.

Follow-Up/Assessment/Extension
- The written assignment will be a good basis for assessment of the students' success with this assignment. Create a rubric explaining the criteria on which their written assignments will be evaluated.
- Tell students to continue observing examples of isolation, and the effects that can result.
- Have some students read/present their writing assignments to the class to practice more speaking/listening skills and to expose all students to each others' ideas.
- Use this assignment to introduce the idea of how oppression and "othering" can have a significant effect on characterization and plot.

Of Mice And Men Chapter 4: What Are The Effects Of Isolation?

Chapter 4 shows the interactions between the novel's most disempowered, oppressed and "othered" characters. While the characters' experiences might give them a sense of empathy for one another, this is not what occurs, and the chapter ends with the barriers created by class, race, gender, and physical/mental disability intact. Each of these characters remains essentially isolated from each other and the others on the ranch. This writing assignment will explore the ideas of loneliness and isolation as a product of prejudice as depicted in the novel.

Using textual evidence from Chapter 4, look for important but perhaps seemingly insignificant details to answer to the question: What are the effects of isolation?

To explore the concept of isolation:

1. Identify passages and quotes which offer details about or insights into the characters' alienation/isolation/loneliness.

2. Examine the context of your quotes.

3. Consider the connotation and denotation of key phrases in your quotes.

    a. How does the character identify or speak about his/her alienation/isolation?
    b. In what ways do characters attempt to overcome this alienation?
    c. In what ways are characters prejudiced towards one another?
    d. How do characters address one another?
    e. Why do they lack empathy for one another? How is this an effect of isolation?

Of Mice And Men Chapter 4: What Are The Effects Of Isolation? Page 2

Use Your Own Knowledge

1. What does isolation/loneliness mean to you?

2. Why are people prejudiced toward one another?

3. What are some effects of being isolated from others?

Of Mice And Men Chapter 4: What Are The Effects Of Isolation? Page 3

Complete as many of these charts as you need to analyze all the information about loneliness, isolation and alienation. Find quotes from the text where characters reveal the effects of their isolation.

Quote (and page number)	Paraphrase Quote	What is revealed about the speaker of the quote?	How is isolation affecting the speaker?

Of Mice and Men Chapter 4
Suggested Writing Assignments

Anchor Standard	8th Grade	9th-10th Grade
CCRA.W.1	W.8.1, 1a-1d	W.9-10.1, 1a-1e
CCRA.W.2	W.8.2, 2a-2f	W.9-10.2, 2a-2f
CCRA.W.3	W.8.3, 3a-3e	W.9-10.3, 3a-3e
CCRA.W.4	W.8.4	W.9-10.4
CCRA.W.5	W.8.5	W.9-10.5

Objective
Students will be assigned or will choose one of a selection of writing assignments pertaining to Chapter 4 of *Of Mice and Men* to fulfill one or more of the standards listed above.

Directions
To provide you with maximum flexibility for differentiated instruction, the following page has a list of suggested writing assignments, all related to Chapter 4 of *Of Mice and Men*. Either assign individual students particular assignments to do or allow students to choose their own assignments.

A second page of "Quick Write" topics is also included.

Follow-Up/Assessment/Extension
- Have dramatic readings of students' narratives or poems.
- Create a "reading room" space in your classroom where students can donate their writing assignments for others in the class to read.
- Allow students to do more than one assignment if they want to.
- Use the "left-over" assignments (not chosen for this activity) as topics for journal entries.

Of Mice And Men Chapter 4: Creative Analytical Writing Assignments

1. Write a flashback scene about Crooks's childhood.

2. Write a scene in dialogue of a conversation between Curley's wife and her friends about her desire to become a movie star.

3. Write a letter from Crooks to his brother that tells about his life on the ranch.

4. What is George's real dream, finding a nice girl? Describe it in a paragraph.

5. Write about ways in which Lennie would be lonely or isolated if George deserted him.

6. Write a letter from Curley's wife to her friend that describes her feelings about her marriage to Curley.

7. Describe the joy the men feel in sharing a dream to start a farm together.

8. Write about what Crooks might have seen, but could not believe his eyes.

9. Rewrite the dialogue as if the men admitted that Lennie broke Curley's hand.

10. Write a paragraph from Lennie's perspective about why he likes rabbits so much.

Of Mice and Men Chapter 4: Quick-Write Writing Assignments

1. Compare Crooks's bunk to the others' bunk.
2. Why does Curley's wife say she is thinking of getting pet rabbits?
3. Are Candy's insults toward Curley's wife justified?
4. Why is it significant that Crooks has more possessions than the others?
5. Why does Curley's wife say she likes talking to Candy, Crooks, and Lennie?
6. Does Candy believe that his word would prevail against Curley's wife about framing Crooks? Why?
7. What is the significance of the mentions of the horses and halters throughout the chapter?
8. In what ways does George act prejudiced?
9. Why is George so angry at the end of the chapter?
10. What do the mentions of Crooks's physical pain signify? Why does the chapter end with an allusion to his physical pain?

NOTES
OF MICE AND MEN

MATERIALS: CHAPTER 5
OF MICE AND MEN

Reading Activity 1: True or False?

Reading Activity 2: Analyzing Passages

Reading Activity 3: Round Characters Or Stereotypes?

Reading Activity 4: Action, Character, Decision

Reading Activity 5: Figurative Language

Reading Activity 6: Elements of Fiction & Literary Devices

Reading Activity 7: Meaning and Inferences

Writing Activity 1: What Does Curley's Wife Symbolize?

Suggested Writing Assignments

Quick-Write Assignments

NOTES
OF MICE AND MEN

Of Mice And Men Chapter 5
Reading Activity 1: True or False

Anchor Standard	8th Grade	9th-10th Grade
CCRA.R.1	RL.8.1	RL.9-10.1
CCRA.SL.1	SL.8.1	SL.9-10.1
CCRA.SL.4	SL.8.4	SL.9-10.4

Objectives
- Students will be able to cite the parts of the text that support their analysis of what the text says or infers.
- Students will consider statements about the text, determine whether those statements are true or false, and will give textual evidence supporting their choices.
- Students will work together in small groups to discuss, analyze, and evaluate the statements made.
- Students will evaluate the analytical work of their peers.

Directions
Prior to reading Chapter 5: Give students (or post) the following list of statements about the chapters, and explain to students that they should read Chapter 5 to find out if these statements are true or false:

Lennie decides to tell George that he found the puppy dead.
Lennie talks easily and freely with Curley's wife.
Curley's wife longs for a different life.
Lennie breaks Curley's wife's neck.
George always believed that he could buy a farm.
George is afraid that he will be implicated in the death of Curley's wife.

After reading Chapter 5: The worksheets on the following pages can be done by students individually, in small groups, or as a whole class. Below are directions to use the questions as a group activity to fulfill more state standards:

- Cut the worksheet apart, making each question and answer box a slip.
- Divide your class into six groups and give one question and a True/False evaluation form to each group. Tell students they are to discuss the statement and determine if the statement is true or false, supporting their decision with evidence from the text. Tell them their answers will be evaluated on the criteria given on the evaluation form.
- Give students ample time to discuss the statements and record their answers.
- Have the groups swap True or False question slips so that each group can evaluate another group's answer. The group should fill in the number of the question they are evaluating, decide how well the answer fulfills the criteria listed, and fill out the form accordingly.
- Repeat the previous step until all the groups have evaluated each others' answers.
- Collect the evaluations and answer slips.

Follow-Up/Assessment/Extension:

- You could average and record the grades each group received for its answers.
- Students could write in their journals or notebooks one thing they learned from this activity.
- You could hold a whole-class discussion about each or any of the statements, either solely orally or using a blank True or False Worksheet on your whiteboard, filling it in as the discussion unfolds.
- At the beginning of the next class, you could hold a brief discussion reviewing the facts addressed by the True/False Worksheet, to see what students have retained and to reinforce the information.
- You could have students make up (and fill in) their own True/False Worksheets for other information located within this chapter.

Of Mice And Men Chapter 5: True or False?

Write *True* or *False* in the blank next to each statement. Below the statement, explain why you chose true or false, referencing the text to support your choices.

_____ 1. Lennie decides to tell George that he found the puppy dead.

_____

_____ 2. Lennie talks easily and freely with Curley's wife.

_____

_____ 3. Curley's wife longs for a different life.

_____

Of Mice And Men Chapter 5 True or False? Page 2

_____ 4. Lennie breaks Curley's wife's neck.

_____ 5. George always believed that he could buy a farm.

_____ 6. George is afraid that he will be implicated in the death of Curley's wife.

Of Mice And Men Chapter 5 True or False? Evaluation

List Your Group's Members: Your Group's Question # _____

_____   _____   _____

_____   _____   _____

1 = No, Not At All **2** = A Little **3** = Some **4** = Yes **5** = Yes, Very Well

Evaluation of Question # ___
Does the explanation support the answer of true or false?   1 2 3 4 5
Is there good textual evidence to support the answer?   1 2 3 4 5
Is the answer clearly stated?   1 2 3 4 5
                    Total Score _____ of a possible 15 points

Evaluation of Question # ___
Does the explanation support the answer of true or false?   1 2 3 4 5
Is there good textual evidence to support the answer?   1 2 3 4 5
Is the answer clearly stated?   1 2 3 4 5
                    Total Score _____ of a possible 15 points

Evaluation of Question # ___
Does the explanation support the answer of true or false?   1 2 3 4 5
Is there good textual evidence to support the answer?   1 2 3 4 5
Is the answer clearly stated?   1 2 3 4 5
                    Total Score _____ of a possible 15 points

Evaluation of Question # ___
Does the explanation support the answer of true or false?   1 2 3 4 5
Is there good textual evidence to support the answer?   1 2 3 4 5
Is the answer clearly stated?   1 2 3 4 5
                    Total Score _____ of a possible 15 points

Evaluation of Question # ___
Does the explanation support the answer of true or false?   1 2 3 4 5
Is there good textual evidence to support the answer?   1 2 3 4 5
Is the answer clearly stated?   1 2 3 4 5
                    Total Score _____ of a possible 15 points

Of Mice And Men Chapter 5: True or False? Suggested Answers

Write *True* or *False* in the blank next to each statement. Below the statement, explain why you chose true or false, referencing the text to support your choices.

<u>TRUE</u> 1. Lennie decides to tell George that he found the puppy dead.

> Lennie speaks directly to the puppy and says that he is afraid that George will not allow him to tend to rabbits. He decides that the death of the puppy is not significant enough to hide in the brush, but he decides to say that he found the dog dead. Finally he decides that "he'll know. George always knows."

<u>FALSE</u> 2. Lennie talks easily and freely with Curley's wife.

> No, he resists and insists that "George says I ain't to have nothing to do with you—talk to you or nothing." She continues and "Lennie was not to be drawn," but she begins to talk about the puppy and soft things, and Lennie cannot resist.

<u>TRUE</u> 3. Curley's wife longs for a different life.

> She tells Lennie "I get awful lonely." She explains to Lennie that she married Curley because she did not receive a letter inviting her to be an actress. She believes strongly that she should have had that life, and is exceedingly miserable on the ranch.

<u>TRUE</u> 4. Lennie breaks Curley's wife's neck.

> Panicked by the woman's screaming, Lennie holds onto her more tightly: "…he shook her; and her body flopped like a fish. And then she was still, for Lennie had broken her neck."

Of Mice And Men Chapter 5: True or False? Suggested Answers Page 2

FALSE 5. George always believed that he could buy a farm.

When Candy asks if they can still get the farm, George replies, "I think I knowed from the very first. I think I knowed we'd never do her." George accepts his fate as a migrant worker as his reality.

TRUE 6. George is afraid that he will be implicated in the death of Curley's wife.

George is afraid that Curley and the others might believe that he colluded with Lennie. He asks Candy to wait to reveal finding Curley's wife and alerting the others. George wants a head start to get to Lennie and handle the situation himself and avoid extreme violence toward Lennie.

Of Mice And Men Chapter 5
Reading Activity 2: Analyzing Passages

Anchor Standard	8th Grade	9th-10th Grade
CCRA.R.6	RL.8.1	RL.9-10.1
	RL.8.3	
	RL.8.4	RL.9-10.4
	RL.8.6	
CCRA.SL.1	SL.8.1	SL.9-10.1

Objectives
- Students will analyze what the text says explicitly as well as inferences drawn from the text.
- Students will analyze how different points of view of the characters creates meaning.
- Students will analyze the impact of specific word choices on meaning and tone.

Directions
On the pages that follow, there are 8 passages to analyze, each with a question or questions to guide the process. There are many ways to use these questions:

- You could use them as a worksheet for all students to complete individually.
- You could use the worksheet as your guide in a whole-class discussion. Have students turn to the first passage in the book, read it, then ask the question(s) orally. Repeat through all 8 questions.
- You could assign one passage to each of 8 different groups of students, for the students to discuss and come up with responses to the question(s). Then hold a whole-class discussion.
- You could read the passage and then see which student can find the passage first (to practice skimming skills). Then follow up with the questions(s) and discussion.
- You could have students choose one or two questions to respond to in writing in their notebooks or journals.

Follow-Up/Assessment/Extension
- Have students write about Curley's wife's sadness. Why is she able to confess her feelings to Lennie?
- Have students pick out other passages in this chapter that show interesting word usage, descriptions, or lack of clarity.
- As an introduction to this activity and this chapter, ask students to write about strength, weakness and vulnerability.

Of Mice And Men Chapter 5 Analyzing Passages

Answer the questions following the quotations completely.

1. He was so little," said Lennie. "I was jus playin' with him... an' he made like he's gonna bite me... an' I made like I was gonna smack him ... an'... an' I done it. An' then he was dead.

She consoled him. "Don't you worry none. He was jus' a mutt. You can get another one easy. The whole country is fulla mutts."

What is the connotation of the last line?

2. "I tell you I ain't used to livin' like this. I coulda made somethin' of myself." She said darkly, "Maybe I will yet." And then her words tumbled out in a passion of communication, as though she hurried before her listener could be taken away. "I lived right in Salinas," she said. "Come there when I was a kid. Well, a show come through, an' I met one of the actors. He says I could go with that show. But my ol' lady wouldn' let me. She says because I was on'y fifteen. But the guy says I coulda. If I'd went, I wouldn't be livin' like this, you bet."

How is Curley's wife's manner of speaking described? Why is that significant?

3. Lennie went back and looked at the dead girl. The puppy lay close to her. Lennie picked it up. "I'll throw him away," he said. "It's bad enough like it is."

What does this suggest about Lennie's capacity to understand what has happened?

Of Mice And Men Chapter 5 Analyzing Passages Page 2

4. "Then—it's all off?" Candy asked sulkily. George didn't answer his question. George said, "I'll work my month an' I'll take my fifty bucks an' I'll stay all night in some lousy cat house. Or I'll set in some poolroom til ever'body goes home. An' then I'll come back an' work another month an' I'll have fifty bucks more."

What does George's response imply?

5. Slim sighed. "Well, I guess we got to get him…"

What is the tone of Slim's statement?

6. "If we could keep Curley in, we might, But Curley's gonna want to shoot 'im. Curley's still mad about his hand. An' s'pose they lock him up an' strap him down and put him in a cage. That ain't no good, George."

According to Slim, what are the biggest threats that face Lennie?

7. And when they were gone, Candy squatted down in the hay and watched the face of Curley's wife. "Poor bastard," he said softly.

To whom is Candy referring?

Of Mice And Men Chapter 5 Analyzing Passages Page 3

8. George said softly, "—I think I knowed from the very first. I think I knowed we'd never do her. He usta like to hear about it so much I got to thinking maybe we would."

What made George believe in the dream?

Of Mice And Men Chapter 5 Analyzing Passages Suggested Answers

Answer the questions following the quotations completely.

1. He was so little," said Lennie. "I was jus playin' with him... an' he made like he's gonna bite me... an' I made like I was gonna smack him ... an'... an' I done it. An' then he was dead.

She consoled him. "Don't you worry none. He was jus' a mutt. You can get another one easy. The whole country is fulla mutts."

What is the connotation of the last line?
Dogs who are "mutts" have no special breeding; they are mixed breeds, often with odd combinations of characteristics. They aren't special like pure bred dogs. The underlying connotation is that the country is full of people who are mutts, like Lennie, George, Candy, Crooks, and Curley's wife…people society marginalizes because they don't measure up to some standard.

2. "I tell you I ain't used to livin' like this. I coulda made somethin' of myself." She said darkly, "Maybe I will yet." And then her words tumbled out in a passion of communication, as though she hurried before her listener could be taken away. "I lived right in Salinas," she said. "Come there when I was a kid. Well, a show come through, an' I met one of the actors. He says I could go with that show. But my ol' lady wouldn' let me. She says because I was on'y fifteen. But the guy says I coulda. If I'd went, I wouldn't be livin' like this, you bet."

How is Curley's wife's manner of speaking described? Why is that significant?
She speaks "darkly," and quickly, as if "her listener could be taken away." She is desperate for a personal connection with someone. To tell her story is a way to validate her existence; she needs to tell someone about her dreams and aspirations.

3. Lennie went back and looked at the dead girl. The puppy lay close to her. Lennie picked it up. "I'll throw him away," he said. "It's bad enough like it is."

What does this suggest about Lennie's capacity to understand what has happened?
Lennie does not understand the gravity of what he has done, but he does understand that he has done something that will displease George and threaten his ability to take care of rabbits, as he decides to dispose of the puppy's body.

4. "Then—it's all off?" Candy asked sulkily. George didn't answer his question. George said, "I'll work my month an' I'll take my fifty bucks an' I'll stay all night in some lousy cat house. Or I'll set in some poolroom til ever'body goes home. An' then I'll come back an' work another month an' I'll have fifty bucks more."

What does George's response imply?
This is his first response to Candy's inquiry. His response—that he will go away, likely until the hubbub around the death of Curley's wife dies down and return to earn the rest of the required money—implies that he continues to believe in the viability of dream.

Of Mice And Men Chapter 5 Analyzing Passages Suggested Answers Page 2

5. Slim sighed. "Well, I guess we got to get him…"

What is the tone of Slim's statement?
Slim continues to be the voice of final authority. The phrase "I guess" shows hesitance and surety simultaneously—he understands that Lennie did not kill out of cruelty, but recognizes that murder, even inadvertent, cannot go unpunished. Fairness and justice must occur.

6. "If we could keep Curley in, we might, but Curley's gonna want to shoot 'im. Curley's still mad about his hand. An' s'pose they lock him up an' strap him down and put him in a cage. That ain't no good, George."

According to Slim, what are the biggest threats that face Lennie?
Slim offers George a realistic perspective. Curley, interestingly, as Slim notes, will be motivated to do maximum harm to Lennie by a sense of revenge for his hand, not necessarily because of the death of his wife. Slim also understands that Lennie's physical strength is a problem, as it will likely mean that he will have to be constrained, which is nearly a total loss of freedom. Death or a life in total captivity are what Lennie faces.

7. And when they were gone, Candy squatted down in the hay and watched the face of Curley's wife. "Poor bastard," he said softly.

To whom is Candy referring?
Candy is not expressing regret for the loss of this woman's life, but for the inevitable damage that the incident causes to Lennie. The way he almost addresses it to Curley's wife's face makes it seem like a reproach to her, as if she victimized Lennie.

8. George said softly, "—I think I knowed from the very first. I think I knowed we'd never do her. He usta like to hear about it so much I got to thinking maybe we would."

What made George believe in the dream?
This passage shows the influence that Lennie has had on George and the value of their friendship and companionship. Lennie's enthusiasm for the story—the myth almost—made George begin to believe it.

Of Mice And Men Chapter 5
Reading Activity 3: Round Characters or Stereotypes?

Anchor Standard	8th Grade	9th-10th Grade
CCRA.R.1	RL.8.1	RL.9-10.1
CCRA.SL.1	SL.8.1	SL.9-10.1

Objective
Using textual evidence, students will explore how characters can be round or stereotyped.

Directions
The round character or stereotype worksheet on the following page could be used in many ways, completed by small groups of students, individual students, or as a whole class activity.

Students will be able to identify which characters in chapter 5 are round character or stereotyped. Students can use their current observations about the characters' growth or absence of growth. Students will think about how plot influences characters and how characters contribute to meaning in the novel. Students can revisit this assignment later in the unit to consider which other characters from earlier in the novel may be stereotypes.

Students may (and should) use their books to skim through the chapter to refresh their memories or gather more information about the characters.

After students complete the worksheets discuss students' answers as a whole class. Collect the worksheets for grading, if you choose, or have students put them in their notebooks for further study.

Follow-Up/Assessment/Extension
Revisit this assignment later in the unit and discuss the relationship between stereotypes and prejudice.

Of Mice And Men Chapter 5
Reading Activity 3: Round Characters or Stereotypes

Characterization in literature can be well developed, creating round characters, or developed in a shallow way relying on generalizations, creating stereotype characters. A stereotype is an over generalized belief about a particular group or class of people. An example of a stereotype is that all kids who play sports get low grades or that all students who get high grades are socially awkward. Round characters often have aspects of their personalities which are unexpected in some way. For example, a teacher in a work of fiction who is a "round character" might also be an Olympic athlete. Stereotyped characters conform to generalized expectations. A teacher in a work of fiction who is stereotyped might be mean, unforgiving and strict.

From the list of characters below, put the names of round characters in the relevant boxes and names of stereotype characters in the relevant boxes. Complete the chart, using actual quotes when asked and noting page numbers. Go back and skim the text if you need to, to refresh your memory about these characters.

Lennie | George | Curley's wife | Slim | Candy | Carlson

Name of Round Character	Quote – Observation 1 (Find a quote that shows how a character has some unexpected quality.)	Quote – Observation 2 (Find a quote that shows how a character has some unexpected quality.)	How do the unexpected qualities shape your understanding of the character?

Name of Stereotype Character	Quote – Observation 1 (Find a quote that shows how a character has a quality that conforms to a stereotype.)	Quote – Observation 2 (Find a quote that shows how a character has a quality that conforms to a stereotype.)	Does the character conform to a stereotype? Describe the stereotype.

Of Mice And Men Chapter 5
Reading Activity 3: Round Characters or Stereotypes Suggested Answers

Characterization in literature can be well developed, creating round characters, or developed in a shallow way relying on generalizations, creating stereotype characters. A stereotype is an over generalized belief about a particular group or class of people. An example of a stereotype is that all kids who play sports get low grades or that all students who get high grades are socially awkward. Round characters often have aspects of their personalities which are unexpected in some way. For example, a teacher in a work of fiction who is a "round character" might also be an Olympic athlete. Stereotyped characters conform to generalized expectations. A teacher in a work of fiction who is stereotyped might be mean, unforgiving and strict.

From the list of characters below, put the names of round characters in the relevant boxes and names of stereotype characters in the relevant boxes. Complete the chart, using actual quotes when asked and noting page numbers. Go back and skim the text if you need to, to refresh your memory about these characters.

Lennie | George | Curley's wife | Slim | Candy | Carlson

Name of Round Character	Quote – Observation 1 (Find a quote that shows how a character has some unexpected quality.)	Quote – Observation 2 (Find a quote that shows how a character has some unexpected quality.)	How do the unexpected qualities shape your understanding of the character?
	To some extent, the definitions of characters as round versus stereotypes is debatable. Lennie could be characterized as either (particularly after chapter 6 when the reader gets a glimpse into Lennie's interior thoughts). George is a round character to some extent as well (especially after the events of chapter 6), as he is a loyal friend but one who is willing to kill his friend out of a sense of mercy and a sense of duty. The remaining characters (Curley's wife/Slim/Candy and Carlson) are largely stereotypes. It could be successfully argued that Curley's wife is a round character; though depicted by the ranchers as a conniving femme fatale, she shows vulnerability and a strong desire to have a different kind of life in chapter 5, even admitting that she does not love Curley.		

Of Mice And Men Chapter 5 Reading Activity 3: Round Characters or Stereotypes Suggested Answers Page 2

Name of Stereotyped Character	Quote – Observation 1 (Find a quote that shows how a character has a quality that conforms to a stereotype.)	Quote – Observation 2 (Find a quote that shows how a character has a quality that conforms to a stereotype.)	Does the character conform to a stereotype? Describe the stereotype.
	Curley's wife/Slim/Candy and Carlson are all stereotyped characters. Curley's wife is the stereotype of a femme fatale, or a dangerous woman. This stereotype is usually shown as being very self-interested and self-absorbed and willing to damage other people's lives to get what they want using any means necessary, including their sexuality. Slim is the classic cowboy, a paragon of American masculinity. Stoic, quiet, competent, strong, moral and just—Slim is all of these things consistently throughout the narrative. Candy is depicted as an invalid—he is dependent on others because of his physical disability. This form of being disempowered means that Candy easily goes along with others, even if he disagrees, like putting down his dog. Carlson is a stereotypical "bindle bum," who lacks a distinct and individual identity and point of view and whose fealty lies with whomever he perceives to have authority.		

Of Mice And Men Chapter 5
Reading Activity 4: Action, Character, Decision

Anchor Standard	8th Grade	9th-10th Grade
CCRA.R.1	RL.8.3	
CCRA.SL.1	SL.8.1	SL.9-10.1

Objective
Students will identify whether particular lines of dialogue or incidents in the story propel the action, reveal aspects of a character, or provoke a decision.

Directions
The following page contains passages from Chapter 5 of Of Mice and Men. Students should determine whether the passages advance the action, reveal aspects of a character, or provoke a decision.

This can be done as a whole-class activity, individually, or in small groups.

Follow-Up/Assessment/Extension
Have students skim Chapter 5 to find one example of a passage that propels the action, one that reveals aspects of a character, and one that provokes a decision. Again, this could be done individually or as a group.

Of Mice and Men Chapter 5: Action, Character, Decision

Write **A** (for Action) **C** (for Character) or **D** (for Decision) in the blank next to each to identify whether the passage/statement advances the action, tells us more about a character, or provokes a decision. On the lines under each question, provide a short explanation of your choice.

____ 1. Suddenly his anger arose. "God damn you," he cried. "Why do you got to get killed? You ain't so little as mice." He picked up the pup and hurled it from him. He turned his back on it. He sat bent over his knees and he whispered, "Now I won't get to tend the rabbits. Now he won't let me." He rocked himself back and forth in his sorrow.

____ 2. Lennie said, "Well, I ain't supposed to talk to you or nothing."

____ 3. "I like to pet nice things. Once at a fair I seen some of them long-hair rabbits. An' they was nice, you bet. Sometimes I've even pet mice, but not when I couldn't get nothing better."

____ 4. "Feel right aroun' there an' see how soft it is." Lennie's big fingers fell to stroking her hair.

____ 5. "That big son-of-a-bitch done it. I know he done it. Why- ever'body else was out there playin' horseshoes." He worked himself into a fury. "I'm gonna get him. I'm going for my shotgun. I'll kill the big son-of-a-bitch myself. I'll shoot 'im in the guts. Come on, you guys." He ran furiously out of the barn. Carlson said, "I'll get my Luger," and he ran out too.

Of Mice And Men Chapter 5:
Action, Character, Decision Suggested Answers

Write **A** (for Action) **C** (for Character) or **D** (for Decision) in the blank next to each to identify whether the passage/statement advances the action, tells us more about a character, or provokes a decision. On the lines under each question, provide a short explanation of your choice.

C 1. Suddenly his anger arose. "God damn you," he cried. "Why do you got to get killed? You ain't so little as mice." He picked up the pup and hurled it from him. He turned his back on it. He sat bent over his knees and he whispered, "Now I won't get to tend the rabbits. Now he won't let me." He rocked himself back and forth in his sorrow.
This passage shows a volatile side of Lennie that is somewhat uncontrolled. His physical strength and lack of judgment (hurling the body of the puppy) make Lennie dangerous and formidable.

D 2. Lennie said, "Well, I ain't supposed to talk to you or nothing."
Lennie knows that he is not supposed to engage in conversation with Curley's wife, and the irony of the passage is that he is speaking to her. She eventually realizes that she can engage him by talking about things he likes—first the puppy and then rabbits and soft things.

C 3. "I like to pet nice things. Once at a fair I seen some of them long-hair rabbits. An' they was nice, you bet. Sometimes I've even pet mice, but not when I couldn't get nothing better."
This passage provides insight into Lennie and his compulsion to touch soft things.

A 4. "Feel right aroun' there an' see how soft it is." Lennie's big fingers fell to stroking her hair.
This key action fuels the most dramatic part of the plot, Lennie's accidental murder of Curley's wife.

D 5. "That big son-of-a-bitch done it. I know he done it. Why- ever'body else was out there playin' horseshoes." He worked himself into a fury. "I'm gonna get him. I'm going for my shotgun. I'll kill the big son-of-a-bitch myself. I'll shoot 'im in the guts. Come on, you guys." He ran furiously out of the barn. Carlson said, "I'll get my Luger," and he ran out too.
Curley makes a decision to take justice into his own hands; he would like to make Lennie suffer ("shoot 'im in the guts" suggests a painful and protracted way to die).

Of Mice and Men Chapter 5
Reading Activity 5: Figurative Language

Anchor Standard	8th Grade	9th-10th Grade
CCRA.R.4	RL.8.4	RL.9-10.4
CCRA.SL.1	SL.8.1	SL.9-10.1

Objectives
- Students will determine the meaning of words and phrases as they are used in the text, including figurative and connotative meanings.
- Students will determine how figurative language contributes to meaning.

Directions
The following page has a passage from the text which includes examples of figurative language. This work-sheet can be done individually, as a whole-class activity, or in small groups. Discuss the answers as a whole class. Collect the worksheets and record the grades if you choose to do so.

Follow-Up/Assessment/Extension
Ask students to begin tracking instances of a particular type of figurative language (personification, metaphor, hyperbole, etc.) in the text. Ask students to make a list to track their observations. Assign students a paper that uses these examples to make an argument about how the language creates meaning.

Of Mice And Men Chapter 5: Figurative Language

Read the following passages, and determine if the language is literal (L), simile (S), metaphor (M), onomatopoeia (O) or hyperbole (H). On the lines below, explain any use of figurative language and the effect it has on meaning.

_____1. The hay came down like a mountain slope to the other end of the barn, and there was a level place as yet unfilled with the new crop.

_____2. "Why can't I talk to you? I never get to talk to nobody. I get awful lonely."

_____3. There was the buzz of flies in the air, the lazy afternoon humming.

_____4. From outside came the clang of horseshoes on the iron stake, and then a little chorus of cries.

_____5. His hair is jus' like wire.

Of Mice And Men Chapter 5: Figurative Language Suggested Answers

Read the following passages, and determine if the language is literal (L), simile (S), metaphor (M), onomatopoeia (O) or hyperbole (H). On the lines below, explain any use of figurative language and the effect it has on meaning.

S 1. The hay came down like a mountain slope to the other end of the barn, and there was a level place as yet unfilled with the new crop.
The placement of the hay is described in comparison to a mountain slope using "like," suggesting that there is a great deal of hay.

H 2. "Why can't I talk to you? I never get to talk to nobody. I get awful lonely."
The statement from Curley's wife that she "never gets[s] to talk to nobody" is an exaggeration, since she can conceivably talk to Curley.

O 3. There was the buzz of flies in the air, the lazy afternoon humming.
"Buzz" is a word that evokes the actual sound that bees make, making it an onomatopoeia.

O 4. From outside came the clang of horseshoes on the iron stake, and then a little chorus of cries.
"Clang" is a word that mimics the sound of metal striking metal, and is an example of onomatopoeia.

S 5. His hair is jus' like wire.
A direct comparison using like is made between wire and hair, making this passage an example of simile.

Of Mice and Men Chapter 5
Reading Activity 6: Elements of Fiction & Literary Devices

Anchor Standard	8th Grade	9th-10th Grade
CCRA.R.1	RL.8.1	RL.9-10.1
	RL.8.2	RL.9-10.2
	RL.8.3	RL.9-10.4
	RL.8.4	RL.9-10.5
	RL.8.6	
CCRA.SL.1	SL.8.1	SL.9-10.1

Objective
Students will study and discuss passages from the text to examine symbol, motif and theme and explore how these create meaning in the text.

Directions
Use the following discussion questions as a guide to discussing symbol, motif and theme, in these chapters. You can give students the questions ahead of time and have them formulate answers prior to the class discussion or you can jump right in with a whole class discussion without student preparation if your students will handle that well.

As you hold the class discussion, be sure to include conversations defining symbol, motif and theme and explaining how these work together to advance meaning in the text.

Follow-Up/Assessment/Extension
After your discussion, ask students to look for recurrences of these symbols, motifs and themes in future chapters.

Of Mice And Men Chapter 5: Elements of Fiction & Literary Devices

One of the primary themes in the novel is fear. Consider the following passages and how Steinbeck presents and defines the concept of fear.

1. Suddenly his anger arose. "God damn you," he cried. "Why do you got to get killed? You ain't so little as mice." He picked up the pup and hurled it from him.

Have similar situations been foreshadowed?

2. Curley's wife came around the end of the last stall. She came very quietly, so that Lennie didn't see her. She wore her bright cotton dress and the mules with the red ostrich feathers. Her face was made up and the little sausage curls were all in place. She was quite near to him before Lennie looked up and saw her.

Curley's wife is a character archetype patterned after the Biblical figure Eve from the story of The Garden of Eden. How does this description of her fit that archetype?

3. Her face grew angry. "Wha's the matter with me?" she cried. "Ain't I got a right to talk to nobody? Whatta they think I am, anyways? You're a nice guy. I don't know why I can't talk to you. I ain't doin' no harm to you."

This passage is very much about prejudice. Why is it ironic?

4. Curley's wife lay with a half-covering of yellow hay. And the meanness and the plannings and the discontent and the ache for attention were all gone from her face. She was very pretty and simple, and her face was sweet and young. Now her rouged cheeks and her reddened lips made her seem alive and sleeping very lightly. The curls, tiny little sausages, were spread on the hay behind her head, and her lips were parted.

What does this description suggest about how women are presented in the novel?

5. As happens sometimes, a moment settled and hovered and remained for much more than a moment. And sound stopped and movement stopped for much, much more than a moment.

How does the passage connect to the theme of nature and cycles?

6. Old Candy watched him go. He looked helplessly back at Curley's wife, and gradually his sorrow and his anger grew into words. "You God damn tramp", he said viciously. "You done it, di'n't you? I s'pose you're glad. Ever'body knowed you'd mess things up. You wasn't no good. You ain't no good now, you lousy tart." He sniveled, and his voice shook. "I could of hoed in the garden and washed dishes for them guys." He paused, and then went on in a singsong. And he repeated the old words: "If they was a circus or a baseball game... we would of went to her... jus' said 'ta hell with work,' an' went to her. Never ast nobody's say so. An' they'd of been a pig and chickens... an' in the winter... the little fat stove... an' the rain comin'... an' us jes' settin' there." His eyes blinded with tears and he turned andwent weakly out of the barn, and he rubbed his bristly whiskers with his wrist stump.

How does this passage relate to the theme of freedom?

Of Mice And Men Chapter 5:
Elements of Fiction & Literary Devices Suggested Answers

One of the primary themes in the novel is fear. Consider the following passages and how Steinbeck presents and defines the concept of fear.

1. Suddenly his anger arose. "God damn you," he cried. "Why do you got to get killed? You ain't so little as mice." He picked up the pup and hurled it from him.

Have similar situations been foreshadowed?
This is a doubling of the incident with the mouse at the beginning of the novel. Lennie lies to George about finding the mouse dead and is also reluctant to give up the mouse when George tells him it is not "fresh." The incident is also echoed later when Lennie breaks Curley's wife's neck.

2. Curley's wife came around the end of the last stall. She came very quietly, so that Lennie didn't see her. She wore her bright cotton dress and the mules with the red ostrich feathers. Her face was made up and the little sausage curls were all in place. She was quite near to him before Lennie looked up and saw her.

Curley's wife is a character archetype patterned after the Biblical figure Eve from the story of The Garden of Eden. How does this description of her fit that archetype?
She is, like the biblical Eve, depicted as a temptress, literally decked out in plumage. Her hair and makeup have been done, and she is completely dressed up to be looked at as an object of desire.

3. Her face grew angry. "Wha's the matter with me?" she cried. "Ain't I got a right to talk to nobody? Whatta they think I am, anyways? You're a nice guy. I don't know why I can't talk to you. I ain't doin' no harm to you."

This passage is very much about prejudice. Why is it ironic?
Sometimes prejudice—or making a determination about something in advance of experiencing it personally—actually keeps people safe. Here Curley's wife suggests that she is "doin' no harm" to Lennie, when, actually, she is. Further, the passage becomes even more ironic when she reflects on how Lennie is nice/harmless, when he is a great unknown danger to her.

4. Curley's wife lay with a half-covering of yellow hay. And the meanness and the plannings and the discontent and the ache for attention were all gone from her face. She was very pretty and simple, and her face was sweet and young. Now her rouged cheeks and her reddened lips made her seem alive and sleeping very lightly. The curls, tiny little sausages, were spread on the hay behind her head, and her lips were parted.

What does this description suggest about how women are presented in the novel?
She is literally described as being out of her misery ("meanness and the plannings and the discontent...gone from her face"). In this state, she is "pretty" and "simple," as if this is the preferred state for women. Further, she is described almost like a film actress, literally a beautiful prop in the scene.

5. As happens sometimes, a moment settled and hovered and remained for much more than a moment. And sound stopped and movement stopped for much, much more than a moment.

How does the passage connect to the theme of nature and cycles?

The passage talks about time as a collection of moments, and the natural imagery Steinbeck depicts also has a seasonality and cycle to it. This passage refers specifically to the moment of Curley's wife's death. The opposite of life and the flow of time is time stopping. The moment itself has created a ripple effect, much like the ripples in the scummy pond that fascinate Lennie. The moment that Curley's wife and Lennie interacted caused a ripple effect that affected the natural cycles of their lives.

6. Old Candy watched him go. He looked helplessly back at Curley's wife, and gradually his sorrow and his anger grew into words. "You God damn tramp", he said viciously. "You done it, di'n't you? I s'pose you're glad. Ever'body knowed you'd mess things up. You wasn't no good. You ain't no good now, you lousy tart." He sniveled, and his voice shook. "I could of hoed in the garden and washed dishes for them guys." He paused, and then went on in a singsong. And he repeated the old words: "If they was a circus or a baseball game... we would of went to her... jus' said 'ta hell with work,' an' went to her. Never ast nobody's say so. An' they'd of been a pig and chickens... an' in the winter... the little fat stove... an' the rain comin'... an' us jes' settin' there." His eyes blinded with tears and he turned and went weakly out of the barn, and he rubbed his bristly whiskers with his wrist stump.

How does this passage relate to the theme of freedom?

Understandably, Candy is bitterly disappointed that the death of Curley's wife has also caused the impossibility of buying a farm. The "old words" he repeats are the ones that primarily highlighted the independence that having a self-sufficient farm would give him. Now, he remains completely dependent on his employer for any semblance of a life that is not marked by the vulnerability of poverty, joblessness, and homelessness.

Of Mice And Men Chapter 5
Reading Activity 7: Meaning and Inferences

Anchor Standard	8th Grade	9th-10th Grade
CCRA.R.1	RL.8.1	RL.9-10.1
CCRA.SL.1	SL.8.1	SL.9-10.1

Objective
Students will answer questions about selected passages from the text which require them to extract meaning or inferences from the text.

Directions
The following pages contain passages from Chapter 5 of *Of Mice and Men* and questions related to the passages that require close reading to answer. Students should answer the questions related to the passages.

This can be done as a whole-class activity, individually, or in small groups. If it is done individually or in small groups, come together as a class to discuss the answers to the questions.

Follow-Up/Assessment/Extension
Collect the worksheets for review and/or grading.

Of Mice And Men Chapter 5: Meaning & Inferences 1

Read the passages and answer the related questions.

1. *She moved closer to him and she spoke soothingly. "Don't you worry about talkin' to me. Listen to the guys yell out there. They got four dollars bet in that tenement. None of them ain't gonna leave till it's over."*

What is the connotation of the word "soothingly"?

2. *"Seems like they ain't none of them cares how I gotta live."*

What is the tone of the passage?

3. *Curley's wife said angrily, "Don't you think of nothing but rabbits?"*

Why does she say it "angrily"?

4. *He moved his hand a little and her hoarse cry came out. Then Lennie grew angry. "Now don't," he said. "I don't want you to yell. You gonna get me in trouble jus' like George says you will. Now don't you do that." And she continued to struggle, and her eyes were wild with terror. He shook her then, and he was angry with her. "Don't you go yellin'," he said, and he shook her; and her body flopped like a fish. And then she was still, for Lennie had broken her neck.*

Compare this passage to the description of Curley's fight with Lennie. What do they share in common? Why is this significant?

5. *Around the last stall came a shepherd bitch, lean and long, with heavy, hanging dugs. Halfway to the packing box where the puppies were she caught the dead scent of Curley's wife, and the hair arose along her spine. She whimpered and cringed to the packing box, and jumped in among the puppies.*

What does the dog's reaction suggest?

Of Mice And Men Chapter 5: Meaning & Inferences 1 Suggested Answers

1. *She moved closer to him and she spoke soothingly. "Don't you worry about talkin' to me. Listen to the guys yell out there. They got four dollars bet in that tenement. None of them ain't gonna leave till it's over."*

What is the connotation of the word "soothingly"?
It has a manipulative overture to it—she wants so desperately to speak to someone that she figures out what Lennie cares about (his puppy and rabbits). It further suggests Curley's wife as a temptress and a woman who ruins men.

2. *"Seems like they ain't none of them cares how I gotta live".*

What is the tone of the passage?
It is hurt and dejected in a real way and a true hunger for empathy. Her ability to have empathy and its absence in her life as the men show her none is signaled by the word "seems"---she tries to see herself from their perspective.

3. *Curley's wife said angrily, "Don't you think of nothing but rabbits?"*

Why does she say it "angrily"?
She is literally starving for attention, which she conceivably can command relatively easily from men, but Lennie's disinterest in her in favor of rabbits is bewildering to her.

4. *He moved his hand a little and her hoarse cry came out. Then Lennie grew angry. "Now don't," he said. "I don't want you to yell. You gonna get me in trouble jus' like George says you will. Now don't you do that." And she continued to struggle, and her eyes were wild with terror. He shook her then, and he was angry with her. "Don't you go yellin'," he said, and he shook her; and her body flopped like a fish. And then she was still, for Lennie had broken her neck.*

Compare this passage to the description of Curley's fight with Lennie. What do they share in common? Why is this significant?
In both passages, Lennie's "victims" are described as fish. This connects the people to the natural world that Steinbeck describes in the Salinas Valley. Just as Curley and his wife are "fish," Lennie is often characterized as bear-like, a natural predator of fish. When bears kill fish, it is part of the natural cycle—it is not exactly murder, just as Lennie's incidents of violence are not malicious. It characterizes Lennie as innocent in an animal-like way.

5. *Around the last stall came a shepherd bitch, lean and long, with heavy, hanging dugs. Halfway to the packing box where the puppies were she caught the dead scent of Curley's wife, and the hair arose along her spine. She whimpered and cringed to the packing box, and jumped in among the puppies.*

What does the dog's reaction suggest?
The novel lacks many references to female characters and this is the only interaction between two female "characters" in the novel. The dog comes around the same stall that Curley's wife did, which makes the reader think of them in a parallel way. The dog's femininity is emphasized ("bitch," "dugs"), and the dog is frightened by her awareness of Curley's wife. The dog's immediate response is maternal, to protect her puppies. This act gives her purpose and (unlike Curley's wife) a legitimate reason to be in the barn.

Of Mice and Men Chapter 5: Meaning & Inferences 2

Read the passage and answer the related questions.

She went on with her story quickly, before she should be interrupted. "'Nother time I met a guy, an' he was in pitchers. Went out to the Riverside Dance Palace with him. He says he was gonna put me in the movies. Says I was a natural. Soon's he got back to Hollywood he was gonna write to me about it." She looked closely at Lennie to see whether she was impressing him. "I never got that letter," she said. "I always thought my ol' lady stole it. Well, I wasn't gonna stay no place where I couldn't get nowhere or make something of myself, an' where they stole your letters. I ast her if she stole it, too, an' she says no. So I married Curley. Met him out to the Riverside Dance Palace that same night." She demanded, "You listenin'?"

"Me? Sure."

"Well, I ain't told this to nobody before. Maybe I oughten to. I don' like Curley. He ain't a nice fella." And because she had confided in him, she moved closer to Lennie and sat beside him. "Coulda been in the movies, an' had nice clothes- all them nice clothes like they wear. An' I coulda sat in them big hotels, an' had pitchers took of me. When they had them previews I coulda went to them, an' spoke in the radio, an' it wouldn'ta cost me a cent because I was in the pitcher. An' all them nice clothes like they wear. Because this guy says I was a natural." She looked up at Lennie, and she made a small grand gesture with her arm and hand to show that she could act. The fingers trailed after her leading wrist, and her little finger stuck out grandly from the rest.

1. How likely were Curley's wife's dreams to happen? Does she believe that they were likely to happen?

2. Why does she care if she is "impressing" Lennie?

3. Why does she marry Curley?

4. Compare the details of the Curley wife's dream to the farm.

Of Mice and Men Chapter 5: Meaning & Inferences 2 Suggested Answers

She went on with her story quickly, before she should be interrupted. "'Nother time I met a guy, an' he was in pitchers. Went out to the Riverside Dance Palace with him. He says he was gonna put me in the movies. Says I was a natural. Soon's he got back to Hollywood he was gonna write to me about it." She looked closely at Lennie to see whether she was impressing him. "I never got that letter," she said. "I always thought my ol' lady stole it. Well, I wasn't gonna stay no place where I couldn't get nowhere or make something of myself, an' where they stole your letters. I ast her if she stole it, too, an' she says no. So I married Curley. Met him out to the Riverside Dance Palace that same night." She demanded, "You listenin'?"

"Me? Sure."

"Well, I ain't told this to nobody before. Maybe I oughten to. I don' like Curley. He ain't a nice fella." And because she had confided in him, she moved closer to Lennie and sat beside him. "Coulda been in the movies, an' had nice clothes- all them nice clothes like they wear. An' I coulda sat in them big hotels, an' had pitchers took of me. When they had them previews I coulda went to them, an' spoke in the radio, an' it wouldn'ta cost me a cent because I was in the pitcher. An' all them nice clothes like they wear. Because this guy says I was a natural." She looked up at Lennie, and she made a small grand gesture with her arm and hand to show that she could act. The fingers trailed after her leading wrist, and her little finger stuck out grandly from the rest.

1. How likely were Curley's wife's dreams to happen? Does she believe that they were likely to happen?
They were unlikely, and the reader should have a sense of that from experience in the real world—many people long for the fame of being an actor or actress and very few achieve matinee idol status. She believed that she deserved for it to happen to her, which is different than believing that it would happen. When she feels that she is unable to accomplish it because forces like her mother intervene, she marries Curley instead.

2. Why does she care if she is "impressing" Lennie?
She derives a sense of self-worth even from just having had the dream and the promise of being an actress, even if she never accomplished it. She uses these stories to garner attention and esteem from people, and it requires their attention. Lennie is not interested in Curley's wife in ways that men likely are drawn to her (her sexuality/body/flirtatiousness) and therefore is not providing her with the reflected glory ("impressing") that she seeks.

3. Why does she marry Curley?
She wanted an alternative to her home life, as she felt that her mother hampered her opportunities to better herself.

4. Compare the details of the Curley wife's dream to the farm.
A reader can intuit by the way she tells her story that it is a story that has been told and embroidered with detail many, many times. The details of the clothing and being a natural resound like "livin' offa tha fat a the land."

Of Mice and Men Chapter 5
Writing Activity 1: What Does Curley's Wife Symbolize?

Anchor Standard	8th Grade	9th-10th Grade
CCRA.SL.1	SL.8.1, 1a-1d	SL.9-10.1, 1a-1d
CCRA.SL.3	SL.8.4	SL.9-10.4
CCRA.W.1	W.8.2	W.9-10.2
CCRA.W.2	W.8.4	W.9-10.4
CCRA.W.4	W.8.5	W.9-10.5
CCRA.W.5		W.9-10.7
		W.9-10.9, 9b

Objectives
- Students will evaluate and analyze textual evidence to uncover how women are depicted in the novel.
- Students will evaluate passages that reveal characterization, motive and conflict.
- Students will examine language for ways in which characterization, motive and conflict illuminate the way that women and femininity is depicted in the novel.
- Students will write a composition in which they consider their analysis of relevant passages to answer the question, "What does Curley's wife symbolize?"

Directions
The following series of worksheets and information organizers can be used by students individually, in small groups, or done partly as a whole-class activity. They are intended to guide students through the process of reading and thinking critically about information by ultimately answering the single question, "What does Curley's wife symbolize?"

Preview the following pages. Determine the best way to have your particular class handle this assignment (individually, pairs, groups, whole-class, or some combination). A combination of group work (to do the analyzing of the text on the chart page) followed by individual work (to do the second and third pages of the assignment) would most likely be best to fulfill the standards listed for this assignment.

Follow-Up/Assessment/Extension
- The written assignment will be a good basis for assessment of the students' success with this assignment. Create a rubric explaining the criteria on which their written assignments will be evaluated.
- Tell students to continue observing examples of isolation, and the effects that can result.
- Have some students read/present their writing assignments to the class to practice more speaking/listening skills and to expose all students to each others' ideas.
- Use this assignment to explore how prevailing cultural norms contemporary to the novel create meaning, and how modern readers can understand the novel in a different context.

Of Mice And Men Chapter 5: "What Does Curley's Wife Symbolize?"

Chapter 5 provides more insight into the only female character who is active and present within the novel. While other women are alluded to—Aunt Clara, the girl in Weed, and madams and prostitutes—only Curley's wife interacts with the novel's protagonists. As seen in Chapter 4, Curley's wife is an isolated character, and the depths of her desperation are explored more fully in Chapter 5 as she converses with Lennie.

Using textual evidence from Chapter 5, look for important but perhaps seemingly insignificant details to answer to the question: What does Curley's wife symbolize?

To define what Curley's wife symbolizes:

1. Identify passages and quotes which offer details about or insights into Curley's wife and her opinions about her past, present and future.

2. Examine the context of your quotes.

3. Consider the connotation and denotation of key phrases in your quotes.

4. Consider these points:
    a. Why does she feel so isolated?
    b. How does she feel about marriage? About Curley?
    c. What dreams does she believe in?
    d. Why is she so angry?
    e. Does she have empathy for Lennie? Did this contribute to the accident?
    f. Does she manipulate Lennie? Did this contribute to the accident?
    g. What do you think Steinbeck would say Curley's wife's role is in the story?
    h. What part of life or society do we see in Curley's wife?

Of Mice And Men Chapter 5: "What Does Curley's Wife Symbolize?" Page 2

Use Your Own Knowledge

1. What were cultural attitudes towards women in the 1930s?

2. What were the cultural expectations for married women in the 1930s?

3. Is Curley's wife a victim of the times she lived in?

Of Mice And Men Chapter 5: "What Does Curley's Wife Symbolize?" Page 3

Complete as many of these charts as you need to explore the symbolism of Curley's wife.

Find a quote about:	Quote (and page number)	Paraphrase Quote	How is isolation affecting the speaker?
Physical description of Curley's wife			
Curley's wife persuading Lennie to talk to her			
Curley's wife's "confessions" to Lennie about her past and her feelings about her marriage			
Others' attitudes or opinions about Curley's wife			

Of Mice And Men Chapter 5
Suggested Writing Assignments

Anchor Standard	8th Grade	9th-10th Grade
CCRA.W.1	W.8.1, 1a-1d	W.9-10.1, 1a-1e
CCRA.W.2	W.8.2, 2a-2f	W.9-10.2, 2a-2f
CCRA.W.3	W.8.3, 3a-3e	W.9-10.3, 3a-3e
CCRA.W.4	W.8.4	W.9-10.4
CCRA.W.5	W.8.5	W.9-10.5

Objective
Students will be assigned or will choose one of a selection of writing assignments pertaining to Chapter 5 of *Of Mice and Men* to fulfill one or more of the standards listed above.

Directions
To provide you with maximum flexibility for differentiated instruction, the following page has a list of suggested writing assignments, all related to Chapter 5 of *Of Mice and Men*. Either assign individual students particular assignments to do or allow students to choose their own assignments.

A second page of "Quick Write" topics is also included.

Follow-Up/Assessment/Extension
- Have dramatic readings of students' narratives or poems.
- Create a "reading room" space in your classroom where students can donate their writing assignments for others in the class to read.
- Allow students to do more than one assignment if they want to.
- Use the "left-over" assignments (not chosen for this activity) as topics for journal entries.

Of Mice and Men Chapter 5: Creative Analytical Writing Assignments

1. Write a flashback scene about Curley's wife's childhood.

2. Write a scene in dialogue of a conversation between Curley's wife and her mother about the probabilities of her dream coming true.

3. Write a scene that depicts Curley and his wife's first meeting.

4. Which dream seems more likely: becoming a movie star or buying a farm?

5. Why does Curley's wife "confess" to Lennie? Was Crooks right about Lennie's being perfect to talk to because he was not capable of retaining information?

6. Why do you think Lennie likes soft things?

7. How startled was Curley's wife by the sight of the dead puppy?

8. Imagine how Candy felt when he realized that buying a farm was unlikely, or more probably, impossible. Write a stream-of-consciousness paragraph about it.

9. Imagine how Curley felt when he realized that Lennie was probably responsible. Write a stream-of-consciousness paragraph about it.

10. Write a paragraph from George's perspective about why Lennie's killing someone was inevitable.

Of Mice and Men Chapter 5: Quick-Write Writing Assignments

1. Why does Curley's wife move so quietly?
2. What motivates Curley's wife to allow Lennie to touch her hair?
3. Is Lennie capable of running away and providing for himself?
4. Why does it matter that the men believe that Lennie stole Carlson's gun?
5. What does Carlson say about shooting Lennie? How does that relate to Candy's dog?
6. Besides George, who else understands exactly what is happening?
7. Is the death of Curley's wife sad?
8. Does Curley seem concerned about his wife's death? Does he seem to have grief about it?
9. How is Curley's wife objectified in the chapter?
10. Is Lennie dangerous? If so, why?

MATERIALS: CHAPTER 6
OF MICE AND MEN

Reading Activity 1: True or False?

Reading Activity 2: Analyzing Passages

Reading Activity 3: A Closer Look At Lennie

Reading Activity 4: Action, Character, Decision

Reading Activity 5: Figurative Language

Reading Activity 6: Elements of Fiction & Literary Devices

Reading Activity 7: Meaning and Inferences

Writing Activity 1: Is Murder An Act Of Friendship?

Suggested Writing Assignments

Quick-Write Assignments

NOTES
OF MICE AND MEN

Of Mice And Men Chapter 6
Reading Activity 1: True or False

Anchor Standard	8th Grade	9th-10th Grade
CCRA.R.1	RL.8.1	RL.9-10.1
CCRA.SL.1	SL.8.1	SL.9-10.1
CCRA.SL.4	SL.8.4	SL.9-10.4

Objectives
- Students will be able to cite the parts of the text that support their analysis of what the text says or infers.
- Students will consider statements about the text, determine whether those statements are true or false, and will give textual evidence supporting their choices.
- Students will work together in small groups to discuss, analyze, and evaluate the statements made.
- Students will evaluate the analytical work of their peers.

Directions
Prior to reading Chapter 6: Give students (or post) the following list of statements about the chapters, and explain to students that they should read Chapter 6 to find out if these statements are true or false:

Aunt Clara is angry at Lennie.
Lennie's greatest fear seems to be George leaving him. Lennie begs George to yell at him.
George is very angry at Lennie.
George kills Lennie out of self-defense.
Slim is understanding and offers George support.

After reading Chapter 6: The worksheets on the following pages can be done by students individually, in small groups, or as a whole class. Below are directions to use the questions as a group activity to fulfill more state standards:

- Cut the worksheet apart, making each question and answer box a slip.
- Divide your class into six groups and give one question and a True/False evaluation form to each group. Tell students they are to discuss the statement and determine if the statement is true or false, supporting their decision with evidence from the text. Tell them their answers will be evaluated on the criteria given on the evaluation form.
- Give students ample time to discuss the statements and record their answers.
- Have the groups swap True or False question slips so that each group can evaluate another group's answer. The group should fill in the number of the question they are evaluating, decide how well the answer fulfills the criteria listed, and fill out the form accordingly.
- Repeat the previous step until all the groups have evaluated each others' answers.
- Collect the evaluations and answer slips.

Follow-Up/Assessment/Extension:
- You could average and record the grades each group received for its answers.
- Students could write in their journals or notebooks one thing they learned from this activity.
- You could hold a whole-class discussion about each or any of the statements, either solely orally or using a blank True or False Worksheet on your whiteboard, filling it in as the discussion unfolds.
- At the beginning of the next class, you could hold a brief discussion reviewing the facts addressed by the True/False Worksheet, to see what students have retained and to reinforce the information.
- You could have students make up (and fill in) their own True/False Worksheets for other information located within this chapter.

Of Mice And Men Chapter 6: True or False?

Write *True* or *False* in the blank next to each statement. Below the statement, explain why you chose true or false, referencing the text to support your choices.

_____ 1. Aunt Clara is angry at Lennie.

_____ 2. Lennie's greatest fear seems to be George's leaving him.

_____ 3. Lennie begs George to yell at him.

Of Mice And Men Chapter 6: True or False? Page 2

_____ 4. George is very angry at Lennie.

_____ 5. George kills Lennie out of self-defense.

_____ 6. Slim is understanding and offers George support.

Of Mice And Men Chapter 6 True or False? Evaluation

List Your Group's Members:	Your Group's Question # _____

_____	_____	_____

_____	_____	_____

1 = No, Not At All **2** = A Little **3** = Some **4** = Yes **5** = Yes, Very Well

Evaluation of Question # ___
Does the explanation support the answer of true or false?	1 2 3 4 5
Is there good textual evidence to support the answer?	1 2 3 4 5
Is the answer clearly stated?	1 2 3 4 5

Total Score _____ of a possible 15 points

Evaluation of Question # ___
Does the explanation support the answer of true or false?	1 2 3 4 5
Is there good textual evidence to support the answer?	1 2 3 4 5
Is the answer clearly stated?	1 2 3 4 5

Total Score _____ of a possible 15 points

Evaluation of Question # ___
Does the explanation support the answer of true or false?	1 2 3 4 5
Is there good textual evidence to support the answer?	1 2 3 4 5
Is the answer clearly stated?	1 2 3 4 5

Total Score _____ of a possible 15 points

Evaluation of Question # ___
Does the explanation support the answer of true or false?	1 2 3 4 5
Is there good textual evidence to support the answer?	1 2 3 4 5
Is the answer clearly stated?	1 2 3 4 5

Total Score _____ of a possible 15 points

Evaluation of Question # ___
Does the explanation support the answer of true or false?	1 2 3 4 5
Is there good textual evidence to support the answer?	1 2 3 4 5
Is the answer clearly stated?	1 2 3 4 5

Total Score _____ of a possible 15 points

Of Mice And Men Chapter 6: True or False? Suggested Answers

Write *True* or *False* in the blank next to each statement. Below the statement, explain why you chose true or false, referencing the text to support your choices.

FALSE 1. Aunt Clara is angry at Lennie.

> Aunt Clara is not actually angry at Lennie, as it is indicated earlier in the novel that she has passed away. Lennie has an episode—it is not completely clear if it is a hallucination or mental illness, and sees and "interacts" with his aunt. She speaks in Lennie's voice and is "disapproving" of him. "Aunt Clara" defends George and accuses Lennie of mistreating him.

TRUE 2. Lennie's greatest fear seems to be George's leaving him.

> Lennie is most disturbed when the gigantic rabbit is trying to convince him that George is "gonna beat hell outta [him]" and "go away and leave." The rabbit repeats over and over "he gonna leave you" and Lennie becomes "frantic." As soon as George arrives, the rabbit "scuttled back." There seems to be a relationship between the two—George helps alleviate Lennie's fear.

TRUE 3. Lennie begs George to yell at him.

> Lennie prompts George to "give [him] hell" multiple times. He knows that it is part of their regular routine—George says these things (going to a cathouse, that life could be so simple) and then they reconcile and things go back to being normal, and Lennie feels secure.

FALSE 4. George is very angry at Lennie.

> Lennie anticipates that George will be angry, a repetition of the first chapter of the novel where George was livid over the incident in Weed. George is not angry this time, and when he does pretend to yell at Lennie, he does it "woodenly." On the verge of shooting Lennie, George underscores to him that he is not mad at him, not now and not ever.

Of Mice And Men Chapter 6: True or False? Suggested Answers Page 2

FALSE 5. George kills Lennie out of self-defense.

George kills Lennie as an act of kindness and protection. He gives a cover story that he killed Lennie out of self-defense and wrestled Carlson's gun away from Lennie, but George was never at risk or endangered.

TRUE 6. Slim is understanding and offers George support.

Despite the cover story that George provides, Slim seems to intuit what actually happened. He sits down next to George, "very close to him." This small detail about proximity suggests that Slim can accomplish an intimate connection of kindness and understanding. Slim also literally helps George to his feet, offering physical support.

Of Mice And Men Chapter 6
Reading Activity 2: Analyzing Passages

Anchor Standard	8th Grade	9th-10th Grade
CCRA.R.6	RL.8.1	RL.9-10.1
	RL.8.3	
	RL.8.4	RL.9-10.4
	RL.8.6	
CCRA.SL.1	SL.8.1	SL.9-10.1

Objectives
- Students will analyze what the text says explicitly as well as inferences drawn from the text.
- Students will analyze how different points of view of the characters and the audience (or reader) creates suspense or humor.
- Students will analyze the impact of specific word choices on meaning and tone.

Directions
On the pages that follow, there are 8 passages to analyze, each with a question or questions to guide the process. There are many ways to use these questions:

- You could use them as a worksheet for all students to complete individually.
- You could use the worksheet as your guide in a whole-class discussion. Have students turn to the first passage in the book, read it, then ask the question(s) orally. Repeat through all 8 questions.
- You could assign one passage to each of 8 different groups of students, for the students to discuss and come up with responses to the question(s). Then hold a whole-class discussion.
- You could read the passage and then see which student can find the passage first (to practice skimming skills). Then follow up with the questions(s) and discussion.
- You could have students choose one or two questions to respond to in writing in their notebooks or journals.

Follow-Up/Assessment/Extension
- Have students write about Curley's wife's sadness. Why is she able to confess her feelings to Lennie?
- Have students pick out other passages in this chapter that show interesting word usage, descriptions, or lack of clarity.
- As an introduction to this activity and this chapter, ask students to write about strength, weakness and vulnerability.

Of Mice And Men Chapter 6 Analyzing Passages

Answer the questions following the quotations completely.

1. She stood in front of Lennie and put her hands on her hips, and she frowned disapprovingly at him.

 And when she spoke, it was in Lennie's voice. "I tol' you an tol' you," she said. "I tol you, 'Min' George because he's such a nice fella an' good to you.' But you don't never take no care. You do bad things."

Why does it matter that it is in Lennie's voice?

2. Lennie said, "George."
"Yeah?"
"I done another bad thing."
"It don't make no difference," George said, and he fell silent again.

What is George's tone?

3. Slim came directly to George and sat down beside him, sat very close to him. "Never you mind," said Slim. "A guy got to sometimes."

To what is Slim referring?

Of Mice And Men Chapter 6 Analyzing Passages Page 2

4. " Lennie said, "I thought you was mad at me, George."
"No," said George. "No, Lennie, I ain't mad. I never been mad, and I ain' now. That's a thing I want ya to know."

What does George's response imply?

5. "The deep green pool of the Salinas River was still in the late afternoon. Already the sun had left the valley to go climbing up the slopes of the Gabilan Mountains, and the hilltops were rosy in the sun. But by the pool among the mottled sycamores, a pleasant shade had fallen."

What is the significance of the light and dark imagery?

6. " Lennie begged, "Le's do it now. Le's get that place now."
"Sure, right now. I gotta. We gotta."
And George raised the gun and steadied it, and he brought the muzzle of it close to the back of Lennie's head. The hand shook violently, but his face set and his hand steadied. He pulled the trigger. The crash of the shot rolled up the hills and rolled down again. Lennie jarred, and then settled slowly forward to the sand, and he lay without quivering."

How does this passage show George's conflict?

Of Mice And Men Chapter 6 Analyzing Passages Page 3

7. But George sat stiffly on the bank and looked at his right hand that had thrown the gun away. The group burst into the clearing, and Curley was ahead. He saw Lennie lying on the sand. "Got him, by God." He went over and looked down at Lennie, and then he looked back at George. "Right in the back of the head," he said softly.

What is Curley's response? Why is it ironic?

8. Curley and Carlson looked after them. And Carlson said, "Now what the hell ya suppose is eatin' them two guys?"

How are George and Slim atypical?

Of Mice And Men Chapter 6 Analyzing Passages Suggested Answers

Answer the questions following the quotations completely.

1. She stood in front of Lennie and put her hands on her hips, and she frowned disapprovingly at him.
 And when she spoke, it was in Lennie's voice. "I tol' you an tol' you," she said. "I tol you, 'Min' George because he's such a nice fella an' good to you.' But you don't never take no care. You do bad things."

Why does it matter that it is in Lennie's voice?
It is important that the image of Aunt Clara has Lennie's voice because it helps the reader see her as a projection of Lennie's mind, rather than a memory. While Aunt Clara may have been parental and instructive toward Lennie, even punishing him at times, she was likely not cruel. So, Lennie being so insistent and cruel toward himself suggests something darker than a lack of intelligence, maybe a version of mental illness. This makes the reader more sympathetic toward Lennie, seeing how much fear and turmoil he experiences personally.

2. Lennie said, "George."
"Yeah?"
"I done another bad thing."
"It don't make no difference," George said, and he fell silent again.

What is George's tone?
George is not at all angry, which is what Lennie anticipated. When George does "give Lennie hell," it is described as "woodenly," "monotonous," and with "no emphasis." His tone is sad, regretful, serious, anticipating that he will shortly be killing his best friend.

3. Slim came directly to George and sat down beside him, sat very close to him. "Never you mind," said Slim. "A guy got to sometimes."

To what is Slim referring?
Slim has been the voice of moral authority, and he can be alluding to the need to subvert the expected process for justice, in favor for what might be more appropriate in a given situation. George has committed a crime and a sin, yet Slim absolves him of guilt for them.

4. " Lennie said, "I thought you was mad at me, George."
"No," said George. "No, Lennie, I ain't mad. I never been mad, and I ain' now. That's a thing I want ya to know."

What does George's response imply?
George's response—explaining that he is not mad now, nor was he ever mad—is a way of making amends and apologizing to Lennie for his treatment of him before taking Lennie's life out of mercy. George is sorry for what he has done and for what he is about to do.

5. "The deep green pool of the Salinas River was still in the late afternoon. Already the sun had left the valley to go climbing up the slopes of the Gabilan Mountains, and the hilltops were rosy in the sun. But by the pool among the mottled sycamores, a pleasant shade had fallen."

What is the significance of the light and dark imagery?
As the chapter moves onward, the shadows and darkness descend. The area by the brush where Lennie is instructed to hide is the first area to go dark, a foreshadowing of the ultimate darkness—death—that Lennie soon will encounter.

6. " Lennie begged, "Le's do it now. Le's get that place now."
"Sure, right now. I gotta. We gotta."
And George raised the gun and steadied it, and he brought the muzzle of it close to the back of Lennie's head. The hand shook violently, but his face set and his hand steadied. He pulled the trigger. The crash of the shot rolled up the hills and rolled down again. Lennie jarred, and then settled slowly forward to the sand, and he lay without quivering."

How does this passage show George's conflict?
The juxtaposition of the much loved and admired dream with the killing shows the conflict and difficulty George faces. George is saying one thing ("Sure…") but meaning another ("I gotta"), implying that he must shoot Lennie immediately.

7. But George sat stiffly on the bank and looked at his right hand that had thrown the gun away. The group burst into the clearing, and Curley was ahead. He saw Lennie lying on the sand. "Got him, by God." He went over and looked down at Lennie, and then he looked back at George. "Right in the back of the head," he said softly.

What is Curley's response? Why is it ironic?
Curley uses the idiom "by God," which is used to emphasize the truth of something. Here Curley believes that his justice—the revenge that he wanted to get on Lennie because Lennie humiliated him and killed his wife—was done. Instead, that is not at all what happened; in fact, George rescues Lennie from the kind of "justice" that Curley wanted to prevail.

8. Curley and Carlson looked after them. And Carlson said, "Now what the hell ya suppose is eatin' them two guys?"

How are George and Slim atypical?
Carlson has no awareness of what has transpired because he has no appreciation of the bond of friendship that men can share. Slim saw that Lennie and George had a caring relationship, and that is why he can relate. Carlson also has no empathy—George just killed someone who was his friend, and Carlson cannot even appreciate the gravity of that.

Of Mice and Men Chapter 6
Reading Activity 3: A Closer Look at Lennie

Anchor Standard	8th Grade	9th-10th Grade
CCRA.R.6	RL.8.1	RL.9-10.1
	RL.8.3	RL.9-10.3

Objectives
- Students will cite textual evidence, analyze it, and draw conclusions from it, specifically regarding the character of Lennie.
- Students will closely analyze the complex character of Lennie, to gain additional insights about him.

Directions
The majority of the novel offers a third person perspective of Lennie. The narrator conveys what Lennie feels but in a way that is moderated.

Chapter 6 is unusual in that it gives insights into Lennie that are radically different from the previous chapters. Lennie's hallucinations of his Aunt Clara and of a giant rabbit are presented as Lennie himself perceives them. This additional information provides characterization for fully understanding Lennie.

Students may (and should) use their books to skim through the chapter to refresh their memories or gather more information about the characters.

After students complete the worksheets discuss students' answers as a whole class. Collect the worksheets for grading, if you choose, or have students put them in their notebooks for further study.

Follow-Up/Assessment/Extension
Revisit this assignment later in the unit and discuss the role that fear plays in the novel as it relates to Lennie.

Of Mice And Men Chapter 6 Reading Activity 3: A Closer Look at Lennie

The majority of the novel offers a third person perspective of Lennie. The narrator conveys what Lennie feels but in a way that is moderated.

Chapter 6 is unusual in that it gives insights into Lennie that are radically different from the previous chapters. Lennie's hallucinations of his Aunt Clara and of a giant rabbit are presented as Lennie himself perceives them. This additional information provides characterization for fully understanding Lennie.

Quote	What does this suggest about Lennie?	How does this portray Lennie in a different way?	Does it make Lennie more or less sympathetic?
Quote that Aunt Clara says			
Quote that Lennie says to Aunt Clara			
Quote that giant rabbit says			
Quote that Lennie says to giant rabbit			

Of Mice And Men Chapter 6
Reading Activity 3: A Closer Look at Lennie Suggested Answers

The majority of the novel offers a third person perspective of Lennie. The narrator conveys what Lennie feels but in a way that is moderated.

Chapter 6 is unusual in that it gives insights into Lennie that are radically different from the previous chapters. Lennie's hallucinations of his Aunt Clara and of a giant rabbit are presented as Lennie himself perceives them. This additional information provides characterization for fully understanding Lennie.

Quote	What does this suggest about Lennie?	How does this portray Lennie in a different way?	Does it make Lennie more or less sympathetic?
Quote that Aunt Clara says Selections will vary	Selections will vary	We see Lennie described as speaking "miserably" and "moan[ing] with grief"	It makes the reader more sympathetic to Lennie; he is not simply forgetful or dumb, but he feels real remorse, fear and sadness that seems profoundly real and disarming to him.
Quote that Lennie says to Aunt Clara Selections will vary	Selections will vary	Lennie expresses that he tried very hard to be better or different.	It makes the reader more sympathetic to Lennie; his subconscious is preoccupied with behaving to please others because he is terrified they will leave him
Quote that giant rabbit says Selections will vary	Selections will vary	The rabbit insults Lennie in the most hurtful way—not only can he not tend the rabbits, but he is "not fit to lick their boots."	The reader sees a scary and sad conflict in Lennie's subconscious. The thing he most wants to have taunts him about being unsuited to have his dream.
Quote that Lennie says to giant rabbit Selections will vary	Selections will vary	Lennie defends George when the rabbit says terrible things about him.	It makes the reader more sympathetic to Lennie, because it shows the deep way that he values George, even if he is not capable of expressing it.

Of Mice and Men Chapter 6
Reading Activity 4: Action, Character, Decision

Anchor Standard	8th Grade	9th-10th Grade
CCRA.R.1	RL.8.3	
CCRA.SL.1	SL.8.1	SL.9-10.1

Objectives
Students will identify whether particular lines of dialogue or incidents in the story propel the action, reveal aspects of a character, or provoke a decision.

Directions
The following page contains passages from Chapter 6 of Of Mice and Men. Students should determine whether the passages advance the action, reveal aspects of a character, or provoke a decision.

This can be done as a whole-class activity, individually, or in small groups.

Follow-Up/Assessment/Extension
Have students skim Chapter 6 to find one example of a passage that propels the action, one that reveals aspects of a character, and one that provokes a decision. Again, this could be done individually or as a group.

Of Mice And Men Chapter 6: Action, Character, Decision

Write **A** (for Action) **C** (for Character) or **D** (for Decision) in the blank next to each to identify whether the passage/statement advances the action, tells us more about a character, or provokes a decision. On the lines under each question, provide a short explanation of your choice.

____ 1. Aunt Clara was gone, and from out of Lennie's head there came a gigantic rabbit.

____ 2. George shook himself again. "No," he said. "I want you to stay with me here."

____ 3. "Go on," said Lennie. "How's it gonna be. We gonna get a little place."

____ 4. "No, Lennie. I ain't mad. I never been mad, an' I ain't now. That's a thing I want ya to know."

____ 5. Slim came directly to George and sat down beside him, sat very close to him.

Of Mice And Men Chapter 6:
Action, Character, Decision Suggested Answers

Write **A** (for Action) **C** (for Character) or **D** (for Decision) in the blank next to each to identify whether the passage/statement advances the action, tells us more about a character, or provokes a decision. On the lines under each question, provide a short explanation of your choice.

C 1. Aunt Clara was gone, and from out of Lennie's head there came a gigantic rabbit.
The inclusion of these terrifying, anxious hallucinations provides further insight into Lennie's character, showing that he is aware of the severity of problems in his life to some extent.

D 2. George shook himself again. "No," he said. "I want you to stay with me here."
As is Lennie's usual practice when George yells at him, he offers to go into the mountains and find a cave and live there so George is unburdened of responsibility. George says that Lennie should stay, but he is really committing to his decision to kill Lennie.

A 3. "Go on," said Lennie. "How's it gonna be. We gonna get a little place."
The sort of ritualistic way that they share the story of their farm aloud is an important part of the final action of the book. George uses the story to create a diversion while he shoots Lennie.

C 4. "No, Lennie. I ain't mad. I never been mad, an' I ain't now. That's a thing I want ya to know."
Here George seems to apologize and pledge his loyalty to his friend. His statement acknowledges past times when he was less than patient and caring, but it also atones for the act he is about to commit.

C 5. Slim came directly to George and sat down beside him, sat very close to him.
Slim's ability to perceive and assess the situation and realize that George killed Lennie out of moral altruism reveals that he too shares these qualities and tendencies, and that he is a moral, good person who can understand and appreciate friendship between men.

Of Mice And Men Chapter 6
Reading Activity 5: Figurative Language

Anchor Standard	8th Grade	9th-10th Grade
CCRA.R.4	RL.8.4	RL.9-10.4
CCRA.SL.1	SL.8.1	SL.9-10.1

Objectives
- Students will determine the meaning of words and phrases as they are used in the text, including figurative and connotative meanings.
- Students will determine how figurative language contributes to meaning.

Directions
The following page has a passage from the text which includes examples of figurative language. This work-sheet can be done individually, as a whole-class activity, or in small groups. Discuss the answers as a whole class. Collect the worksheets and record the grades if you choose to do so.

Follow-Up/Assessment/Extension
Ask students to begin tracking instances of a particular type of figurative language (personification, metaphor, hyperbole, etc.) in the text. Ask students to make a list to track their observations. Assign students a paper that uses these examples to make an argument about how the language creates meaning.

Of Mice And Men Chapter 6: Figurative Language

Read the following passages, and determine if the language is literal (L), simile (S), metaphor (M), personification (P) or hyperbole (H). On the lines below, explain any use of figurative language and the effect it has on meaning.

_____1. A far rush of wind sounded and a gust drove through the tops of the trees like a wave.

_____2. Another little water snake swam up the pool, turning its periscope head from side to side.

_____3. It sat on its haunches in front of him, and it waggled its ears and crinkled its nose at him. And it spoke in Lennie's voice too.

_____4. "You ain't worth a greased jack-pin to ram you into hell.

_____5. George let himself be helped to his feet.

Of Mice And Men Chapter 6: Figurative Language Suggested Answers

Read the following passages, and determine if the language is literal (L), simile (S), metaphor (M), personification (P) or hyperbole (H). On the lines below, explain any use of figurative language and the effect it has on meaning.

S 1. A far rush of wind sounded and a gust drove through the tops of the trees like a wave.
Using "like," Steinbeck compares the way that air moves to the flow of a wave.

M 2. Another little water snake swam up the pool, turning its periscope head from side to side.
Here the word "periscope" works like a metaphor, comparing the instrument on a submarine that allows sailors to glimpse at the surface to a snake.

L 3. It sat on its haunches in front of him, and it waggled its ears and crinkled its nose at him. And it spoke in Lennie's voice too.
Even though the passage refers to a bizarre hallucination, it is literal. A rabbit waggles its ears and crinkles its nose, so it is not hyperbole.

H 4. "You ain't worth a greased jack-pin to ram you into hell.
This is an exaggeration (and a terribly cruel insult), so it's an example of hyperbole.

L 5. George let himself be helped to his feet.
This is literal. It is in the passive voice, so it is phrased a bit unusually, but people are helped to their feet.

Of Mice And Men Chapter 6
Reading Activity 6: Elements of Fiction & Literary Devices

Anchor Standard	8th Grade	9th-10th Grade
CCRA.R.1	RL.8.1	RL.9-10.1
	RL.8.2	RL.9-10.2
	RL.8.3	RL.9-10.4
	RL.8.4	RL.9-10.5
	RL.8.6	
CCRA.SL.1	SL.8.1	SL.9-10.1

Objective
Students will study and discuss passages from the text to examine symbol, motif and theme and explore how these create meaning in the text.

Directions
Use the following discussion questions as a guide to discussing symbol, motif and theme, in these chapters. You can give students the questions ahead of time and have them formulate answers prior to the class discussion or you can jump right in with a whole class discussion without student preparation if your students will handle that well.

As you hold the class discussion, be sure to include conversations defining symbol, motif and theme and explaining how these work together to advance meaning in the text.

Follow-Up/Assessment/Extension
After your discussion, ask students to look for recurrences of these symbols, motifs and themes in future chapters.

Of Mice And Men Chapter 6: Elements of Fiction & Literary Devices

One of the elements of fiction is setting, or the time and place in which action occurs. Consider the quotes below and answer questions about the significance of the setting.

1. The deep green pool of the Salinas River was still in the late afternoon. Already the sun had left the valley to go climbing up the slopes of the Gabilan Mountains, and the hilltops were rosy in the sun. But by the pool among the mottled sycamores, a pleasant shade had fallen.

What does the relationship of sun and shade to the hiding place suggest about the novel's denouement?

2. A water snake glided smoothly up the pool, twisting its periscope head from side to side; and it swam the length of the pool and came to the legs of a motionless heron that stood in the shallows. A silent head and beak lanced down and plucked it out by the head, and the beak swallowed the little snake while its tail waved frantically.

What is the significance of this detail? What themes does it relate to?

3. Suddenly Lennie appeared out of the brush, and he came as silently as a creeping bear moves. The heron pounded the air with its wings, jacked itself clear of the water and flew off down river. The little snake slid in among the reeds at the pool's side.

What is Lennie's relationship to the landscape, according to the text?

Of Mice And Men Chapter 6: Elements of Fiction & Literary Devices Page 2

4. Only the topmost ridges were in the sun now. The shadow in the valley was blue and soft. From the distance came the sound of men shouting to one another. George turned his head and listened to the shouts.

The shifting of the light parallels what action occurring in the text?

5. Lennie removed his hat dutifully and laid it on the ground in front of him. The shadow in the valley was bluer, and the evening came fast. On the wind the sound of crashing in the brush came to them.

What does the wind signify here? What "message" does it deliver?

6. And George raised the gun and steadied it, and he brought the muzzle of it close to the back of Lennie's head. The hand shook violently, but his face set and his hand steadied. He pulled the trigger. The crash of the shot rolled up the hills and rolled down again. Lennie jarred, and then settled slowly forward to the sand, and he lay without quivering.

How and why does a mention of the landscape interrupt the narration of Lennie's death?

Of Mice And Men Chapter 6:
Elements of Fiction & Literary Devices Suggested Answers

One of the elements of fiction is setting, or the time and place in which action occurs. Consider the quotes below and answer questions about the significance of the setting.

1. The deep green pool of the Salinas River was still in the late afternoon. Already the sun had left the valley to go climbing up the slopes of the Gabilan Mountains, and the hilltops were rosy in the sun. But by the pool among the mottled sycamores, a pleasant shade had fallen.

What does the relationship of sun and shade to the hiding place suggest about the novel's denouement?
Throughout the novel Steinbeck has played with light and dark imagery, particularly leading to the deaths of Curley's wife and Lennie. Lennie is now hiding in the brush, and is associated with the natural world. The denouement is foreshadowed, and Lennie's death is imminent. His life is now in shade—but it is "pleasant," as his death will be quick while he is thinking pleasant thoughts about the farm dream.

2. A water snake glided smoothly up the pool, twisting its periscope head from side to side; and it swam the length of the pool and came to the legs of a motionless heron that stood in the shallows. A silent head and beak lanced down and plucked it out by the head, and the beak swallowed the little snake while its tail waved frantically.

What is the significance of this detail? What themes does it relate to?
This detail connects to themes of cycles in the natural world and the relationship between the weak and powerful. Death is a natural part of life, and is seen in the microcosm of nature in the brush. Curley's wife and Lennie are not unlike the snake, weaker than the mightier heron.

3. Suddenly Lennie appeared out of the brush, and he came as silently as a creeping bear moves. The heron pounded the air with its wings, jacked itself clear of the water and flew off down river. The little snake slid in among the reeds at the pool's side.

What is Lennie's relationship to the landscape, according to the text?
Lennie is described as animal like—particularly as a bear—at multiple points in the novel. Fleeing the ranch, the problems he has caused, and the lynching he is facing, Lennie is now more a part of the landscape than he is a citizen of society. Lennie is too innocent to be part of society, which would ultimately harm him.

4. Only the topmost ridges were in the sun now. The shadow in the valley was blue and soft. From the distance came the sound of men shouting to one another. George turned his head and listened to the shouts.

The shifting of the light parallels what action occurring in the text?
As a continuation of the light and dark motif, the conclusion of Lennie's life occurs in shadow. Darkness symbolizes looming danger and death in the novel, and the rising darkness parallels the inevitability of Lennie's death.

Of Mice And Men Chapter 6: Elements of Fiction & Literary Devices Suggested Answers Page 2

5. Lennie removed his hat dutifully and laid it on the ground in front of him. The shadow in the valley was bluer, and the evening came fast. On the wind the sound of crashing in the brush came to them.

What does the wind signify here? What "message" does it deliver?
The wind is a natural element, part of the world that Lennie inhabits as an innocent person; here the wind is what unites the natural world and the organized world of society and law. The wind is what alerts George of the proximity of the lynching party, so in some ways, the wind—a force of nature—delivers Lennie from the violence of revenge-fueled society.

6. And George raised the gun and steadied it, and he brought the muzzle of it close to the back of Lennie's head. The hand shook violently, but his face set and his hand steadied. He pulled the trigger. The crash of the shot rolled up the hills and rolled down again. Lennie jarred, and then settled slowly forward to the sand, and he lay without quivering.

How and why does a mention of the landscape interrupt the narration of Lennie's death?
Steinbeck mentions that the "crash of the shot rolled up the hills and rolled down again." The sound is temporary and it moves up the hills but does not leave the pastoral landscape. Ultimately Lennie rests on the sand, which is consistent with his depiction as bear-like. Lennie finally becomes part of the natural world in his death.

Of Mice and Men Chapter 6
Reading Activity 7: Meaning and Inferences

Anchor Standard	8th Grade	9th-10th Grade
CCRA.R.1	RL.8.1	RL.9-10.1
CCRA.SL.1	SL.8.1	SL.9-10.1

Objective
Students will answer questions about selected passages from the text which require them to extract meaning or inferences from the text.

Directions
The following pages contain passages from Chapter 6 of *Of Mice and Men* and questions related to the passages that require close reading to answer. Students should answer the questions related to the passages.

This can be done as a whole-class activity, individually, or in small groups. If it is done individually or in small groups, come together as a class to discuss the answers to the questions.

Follow-Up/Assessment/Extension
Collect the worksheets for review and/or grading.

Of Mice And Men Chapter 6: Meaning & Inferences 1

Read the passages and answer the related questions.

1. *And then from out of Lennie's head there came a little fat old woman. She wore thick bull's-eye glasses and she wore a huge gingham apron with pockets, and she was starched and clean. She stood in front of Lennie and put her hands on her hips, and she frowned disapprovingly at him.*

What was Aunt Clara probably like in real life?

2. *"Tend rabbits," it said scornfully. "You crazy bastard. You ain't fit to lick the boots of no rabbit. You'd forget 'em and let 'em go hungry. That's what you'd do. An' then what would George think?"*

How does the rabbit offend Lennie? What is the ultimate offense?

3. *But the rabbit repeated softly over and over, "He gonna leave you, ya crazy bastard. He gonna leave ya all alone. He gonna leave ya crazy bastard."*

What is the effect of the repetition?

4. *"Sure, like you always done before. Like, 'If I di'n't have you I'd take my fifty bucks-'"*

Why is it significant that Lennie quotes George?

Of Mice And Men Chapter 6: Meaning & Inferences 1 Page 2

5. *"No, Lennie. Look down there acrost the river, like you can almost see the place."*
Lennie obeyed him. George looked down at the gun. There were crashing footsteps in the brush now. George turned and looked toward them.
"Go on, George. When we gonna do it?"
"Gonna do it soon."
"Me an' you."
"You... an' me. Ever'body gonna be nice to you. Ain't gonna be no more trouble. Nobody gonna hurt nobody nor steal from 'em."

Does Lennie achieve the dream?

Of Mice and Men Chapter 6: Meaning & Inferences 1 Suggested Answers

Read the passages and answer the related questions.

1. *And then from out of Lennie's head there came a little fat old woman. She wore thick bull's-eye glasses and she wore a huge gingham apron with pockets, and she was starched and clean. She stood in front of Lennie and put her hands on her hips, and she frowned disapprovingly at him.*

What was Aunt Clara probably like in real life?
Aunt Clara was likely a parental figure and was disapproving of Lennie when he did things that could cause him harm. She was likely not at all as stringent and unkind as she is depicted in Lennie's imagination. As she has his voice, it suggests that it is the way he may have perceived her—and his view of her may not be accurate.

2. *"Tend rabbits," it said scornfully. "You crazy bastard. You ain't fit to lick the boots of no rabbit. You'd forget 'em and let 'em go hungry. That's what you'd do. An' then what would George think?"*

How does the rabbit offend Lennie? What is the ultimate offense?
The rabbit is the object of Lennie's greatest desire—to care for them and feel their soft fur. Here the rabbit not only says that Lennie cannot tend rabbits (a situation that has recurred many times in the novel), but that he is not worthy of being near rabbits. Effectively, the rabbit tells Lennie that his dream is wrong and impossible and dead.

3. *But the rabbit repeated softly over and over, "He gonna leave you, ya crazy bastard. He gonna leave ya all alone. He gonna leave ya crazy bastard."*

What is the effect of the repetition?
It is terrifying and manic. The reiterations make it seem final and irrevocable. It shows how deeply affected and disturbed Lennie is.

4. *"Sure, like you always done before. Like, 'If I di'n't have you I'd take my fifty bucks—'"*

Why is it significant that Lennie quotes George?
Similar to the way that Lennie quotes the "fatta th' lan'" story, it suggests that their relationship has a script that they played out over and over. It connects their relationship to the dream of the farm, suggesting that their friendship is a similar, rare and nearly unattainable thing.

Of Mice And Men Chapter 6: Meaning & Inferences 1 Suggested Answers Page 2

5. *"No, Lennie. Look down there acrost the river, like you can almost see the place."*
Lennie obeyed him. George looked down at the gun. There were crashing footsteps in the brush now. George turned and looked toward them.
"Go on, George. When we gonna do it?"
"Gonna do it soon."
"Me an' you."
"You... an' me. Ever'body gonna be nice to you. Ain't gonna be no more trouble. Nobody gonna hurt nobody nor steal from 'em."

Does Lennie achieve the dream?
The answer is debatable, but the text suggests that Lennie can see the farm and that he focuses his belief so intensely that it is extant and urgent and as close to attaining the dream as possible.

Of Mice And Men Chapter 6: Meaning & Inferences 2

Read the passage and answer the related questions.

George came quietly out of the brush and the rabbit scuttled back into Lennie's brain.
George said quietly, "What the hell you yellin' about?"
Lennie got up on his knees. "You ain't gonna leave me, are ya, George? I know you ain't."
George came stiffly near and sat down beside him. "No."
"I knowed it," Lennie cried. "You ain't that kind."
George was silent.
Lennie said, "George."
"Yeah?"
"I done another bad thing."
"It don't make no difference," George said, and he fell silent again.
Only the topmost ridges were in the sun now. The shadow in the valley was blue and soft. From the distance came the sound of men shouting to one another. George turned his head and listened to the shouts.
Lennie said, "George."
"Yeah?"
"Ain't you gonna give me hell?"
"Give ya hell?"
"Sure, like you always done before. Like, 'If I di'n't have you I'd take my fifty bucks-'"
"Jesus Christ, Lennie! You can't remember nothing that happens, but you remember ever' word I say."
"Well, ain't you gonna say it?"
George shook himself. He said woodenly, "If I was alone I could live so easy." His voice was monotonous, had no emphasis. "I could get a job an' not have no mess." He stopped.
"Go on," said Lennie. "An' when the enda the month come-"
"An' when the end of the month came I could take my fifty bucks an' go to a... cat house..." He stopped again.
Lennie looked eagerly at him. "Go on, George. Ain't you gonna give me no more hell?"
"No," said George.
"Well, I can go away," said Lennie. "I'll go right off in the hills an' find a cave if you don' want me."
George shook himself again. "No," he said. "I want you to stay with me here."

1. If George's presence makes the rabbit disappear, what does that suggest about the rabbit? About Lennie's relationship with George?

2. Compare this passage to the opening scene of the novel. Why is George's silence here noteworthy?

3. Why does Lennie want George to yell at him?

4. What is the tone of George's reproach? If he doesn't want to yell at Lennie, why does he do it?

Of Mice And Men Chapter 6: Meaning & Inferences 2 Suggested Answers

George came quietly out of the brush and the rabbit scuttled back into Lennie's brain.
George said quietly, "What the hell you yellin' about?"
Lennie got up on his knees. "You ain't gonna leave me, are ya, George? I know you ain't."
George came stiffly near and sat down beside him. "No."
"I knowed it," Lennie cried. "You ain't that kind."
George was silent.
Lennie said, "George."
"Yeah?"
"I done another bad thing."
"It don't make no difference," George said, and he fell silent again.
Only the topmost ridges were in the sun now. The shadow in the valley was blue and soft. From the distance came the sound of men shouting to one another. George turned his head and listened to the shouts.
Lennie said, "George."
"Yeah?"
"Ain't you gonna give me hell?"
"Give ya hell?"
"Sure, like you always done before. Like, 'If I di'n't have you I'd take my fifty bucks-'"
"Jesus Christ, Lennie! You can't remember nothing that happens, but you remember ever' word I say."
"Well, ain't you gonna say it?"
George shook himself. He said woodenly, "If I was alone I could live so easy." His voice was monotonous, had no emphasis. "I could get a job an' not have no mess." He stopped.
"Go on," said Lennie. "An' when the enda the month come-"
"An' when the end of the month came I could take my fifty bucks an' go to a... cat house..." He stopped again.
Lennie looked eagerly at him. "Go on, George. Ain't you gonna give me no more hell?"
"No," said George.
Well, I can go away," said Lennie. "I'll go right off in the hills an' find a cave if you don' want me."
George shook himself again. "No," he said. "I want you to stay with me here."

1. If George's presence makes the rabbit disappear, what does that suggest about the rabbit? About Lennie's relationship with George?
The rabbit embodies Lennie's greatest fears and anxieties. George's companionship helps Lennie feel secure, and, hence, makes the rabbit disappear.

2. Compare this passage to the opening scene of the novel. Why is George's silence here noteworthy?
At the beginning of the novel, George is demonstrably angry, and he takes his frustration out on Lennie. The verbal sparring between the two turns out to be part of their routine, and a step toward things going back to "normal." George's silence is disarming to Lennie, who actually begs to be yelled at because he knows what George will say and that George will cool down and never abandon him.

3. Why does Lennie want George to yell at him?
To Lennie, it is part of a familiar routine and a way that George ultimately confirms his friendship and loyalty to Lennie.

4. What is the tone of George's reproach? If he doesn't want to yell at Lennie, why does he do it?
George yells at Lennie as a way to soothe and reassure him. George does not want to do it because he knows what his actual intentions toward Lennie are to take his life as a way to protect him.

Of Mice And Men Chapter 6
Writing Activity 1: Is Murder An Act Of Friendship?

Anchor Standard	8th Grade	9th-10th Grade
CCRA.SL.1	SL.8.1, 1a-1d	SL.9-10.1, 1a-1d
CCRA.SL.3	SL.8.4	SL.9-10.4
CCRA.W.1	W.8.2	W.9-10.2
CCRA.W.2	W.8.4	W.9-10.4
CCRA.W.4	W.8.5	W.9-10.5
CCRA.W.5		W.9-10.7
		W.9-10.9, 9b

Objectives
- Students will evaluate and analyze textual evidence to interrogate the theme of friendship.
- Students will evaluate passages that reveal characterization, motive and conflict.
- Students will examine language for ways in which characterization, motive and conflict redefine the concept of friendship.
- Students will write a composition in which they consider their analysis of relevant passages to answer the question, "Is murder an act of friendship?"

Directions
The following series of worksheets and information organizers can be used by students individually, in small groups, or done partly as a whole-class activity. They are intended to guide students through the process of reading and thinking critically about information by ultimately answering the single question, "Is murder an act of friendship?"

Preview the following pages. Determine the best way to have your particular class handle this assignment (individually, pairs, groups, whole-class, or some combination). A combination of group work (to do the analyzing of the text on the chart page) followed by individual work (to do the second and third pages of the assignment) would most likely be best to fulfill the standards listed for this assignment.

Follow-Up/Assessment/Extension
- The written assignment will be a good basis for assessment of the students' success with this assignment. Create a rubric explaining the criteria on which their written assignments will be evaluated.
- Tell students to continue observing examples of isolation, and the effects that can result.
- Have some students read/present their writing assignments to the class to practice more speaking/listening skills and to expose all students to each others' ideas.
- Use this assignment to explore how themes in literature can challenge cultural ideas about how people behave in society.

Of Mice And Men Chapter 6: "Is Murder An Act Of Friendship?"

Write a paper in which you analyze the following statement and take a position in agreement with or in opposition to it:

George kills Lennie in the final scene of the novel as an act of friendship.

To evaluate the statement:

1. Identify passages and quotes which offer details about or insights into Steinbeck's notions of friendship.
    - How do Lennie and George define their friendship
    - Lennie and George
        - The boss's and Curley's reaction to their friendship
        - Slim's reaction to their friendship

2. Examine the context of your quotes.

3. Consider the connotation and denotation of key phrases in your quotes.

    a. What does George gain through his friendship with Lennie?
    b. What does Lennie gain through his friendship with George?
    c. What makes the friendship challenging for George?
    d. What makes the friendship challenging for Lennie?
    e. What alternatives does George have?

Of Mice And Men Chapter 6: "Is Murder An Act Of Friendship?" Page 2

Use Your Own Knowledge

1. How do you think most people define friendship?

2. What responsibility does one friend have for another?

3. What is Lennie's greatest fear? How does George's decision relate to it?

Of Mice And Men Chapter 6: "Is Murder An Act Of Friendship?" Page 3

Complete as many of these charts as you need to explore the concept of friendship. In the final scene between George and Lennie, George says and does things but intends a different meaning. Find moments from the text when these double or unintended meanings occur.

Quote (and page number)	Paraphrase Quote	What is its intended meaning?	What is its double/unintended meaning? (What is George actually saying/conveying?)
Example: George took off his hat. He said shakily, "Take off your hat, Lennie. The air feels fine."	Lennie, take off your hat.	That Lennie would enjoy feeling the evening air.	He is preparing to shoot Lennie and finds a gentle and misleading way to get Lennie ready.

Of Mice And Men Chapter 6
Suggested Writing Assignments

Anchor Standard	8th Grade	9th-10th Grade
CCRA.W.1	W.8.1, 1a-1d	W.9-10.1, 1a-1e
CCRA W.2	W.8.2, 2a-2f	W.9-10.2, 2a-2f
CCRA.W.3	W.8.3, 3a-3e	W.9-10.3, 3a-3e
CCRA.W.4	W.8.4	W.9-10.4
CCRA.W.5	W.8.5	W.9-10.5

Objective
Students will be assigned or will choose one of a selection of writing assignments pertaining to Chapter 6 of *Of Mice and Men* to fulfill one or more of the standards listed above.

Directions
To provide you with maximum flexibility for differentiated instruction, the following page has a list of suggested writing assignments, all related to Chapter 6 of *Of Mice and Men*. Either assign individual students particular assignments to do or allow students to choose their own assignments.

A second page of "Quick Write" topics is also included.

Follow-Up/Assessment/Extension
- Have dramatic readings of students' narratives or poems.
- Create a "reading room" space in your classroom where students can donate their writing assignments for others in the class to read.
- Allow students to do more than one assignment if they want to.
- Use the "left-over" assignments (not chosen for this activity) as topics for journal entries.

Of Mice And Men Chapter 6: Creative Analytical Writing Assignments

1. Write a scene of dialogue between Lennie and "Aunt Clara" at a different point in the novel.

2. Write a scene of dialogue between Lennie and "the gigantic rabbit" at a different point in the novel.

3. Write a stream of consciousness paragraph about the thought racing through George's mind as he shoots Lennie.

4. Write a eulogy for Lennie from George's perspective.

5. Write an epilogue that explains if George ever believed in the dream again.

6. Study the Robert Burns poem from which the novel borrows its title. Write a poem inspired by the novel.

7. Write the final scene from a different character's perspective (Slim, Carlson or Curley).

8. Write the final scene from the perspective of the landscape. What do the heron, snake and birds see?

9. Write a newspaper article about Lennie's death.

10. Describe how Lennie was like a bear. What animal is George like?

Of Mice And Men Chapter 6: Quick-Write Writing Assignments

1. Why did George kill Lennie?
2. Why does Lennie beg George to yell at him?
3. What is George's tone toward Lennie?
4. Is Lennie "nuts," as Crooks suggested earlier in the novel?
5. Does Lennie achieve the dream?
6. What is the most suspenseful moment of the novel?
7. Compare Slim and Carlson.
8. Does George's act of killing provide justice?
9. Do any of the characters actually understand friendship?
10. Why is it significant that the novel ends in the place where it began?

NOTES
OF MICE AND MEN

MATERIALS: OVERVIEW
OF MICE AND MEN

Reading Activity 1: True or False?

Reading Activity 2: Analyzing Passages

Reading Activity 3: Characters, Motivation, and Dreams

Reading Activity 4: Action, Character, Decision

Reading Activity 5: Figurative Language

Reading Activity 6: Elements of Fiction & Literary Devices

Reading Activity 7: Meaning and Inferences

Writing Activity 1: Is Sharing A Common Dream Possible?

Suggested Writing Assignments

Quick-Write Assignments

NOTES
OF MICE AND MEN

Of Mice And Men Overview
Reading Activity 1: True or False?

Anchor Standard	8th Grade	9th-10th Grade
CCRA.R.1	RL.8.1	RL.9-10.1
CCRA.SL.1	SL.8.1	SL.9-10.1
CCRA.SL.4	SL.8.4	SL.9-10.4

Objectives
- Students will be able to cite the parts of the text that support their analysis of what the text says or infers.
- Students will consider statements about the text, determine whether those statements are true or false, and will give textual evidence supporting their choices.
- Students will work together in small groups to discuss, analyze, and evaluate the statements made.
- Students will evaluate the analytical work of their peers.

Directions
Prior to reading Novel Overview: Give students (or post) the following list of statements about the chapters, and explain to students that they should read the novel to find out if these statements are true or false:

> Lennie stole Carlson's gun.
> Candy lost his hand in a farming accident.
> George almost caused Lennie to drown.
> Candy is threatened with being lynched.
> George admits to himself that he always knew the dream was unattainable.
> Slim believes that George's killing of Lennie is irresponsible.

After reading Novel Overview: The worksheets on the following pages can be done by students individually, in small groups, or as a whole class. Below are directions to use the questions as a group activity to fulfill more state standards:

- Cut the worksheet apart, making each question and answer box a slip.
- Divide your class into six groups and give one question and a True/False evaluation form to each group. Tell students they are to discuss the statement and determine if the statement is true or false, supporting their decision with evidence from the text. Tell them their answers will be evaluated on the criteria given on the evaluation form.
- Give students ample time to discuss the statements and record their answers.
- Have the groups swap True or False question slips so that each group can evaluate another group's answer. The group should fill in the number of the question they are evaluating, decide how well the answer fulfills the criteria listed, and fill out the form accordingly.
- Repeat the previous step until all the groups have evaluated each other's' answers.
- Collect the evaluations and answer slips.

Of Mice And Men Overview True or False? Page 2

Follow-Up/Assessment/Extension:
- You could average and record the grades each group received for its answers.
- Students could write in their journals or notebooks one thing they learned from this activity.
- You could hold a whole-class discussion about each or any of the statements, either solely orally or using a blank True or False Worksheet on your whiteboard, filling it in as the discussion unfolds.
- At the beginning of the next class, you could hold a brief discussion reviewing the facts addressed by the True/False Worksheet, to see what students have retained and to reinforce the information.
- You could have students make up (and fill in) their own True/False Worksheets for other information located within this chapter.

Of Mice And Men Overview True or False? Evaluation

List Your Group's Members: Your Group's Question # _____

_____   _____   _____

_____   _____   _____

1 = No, Not At All **2** = A Little **3** = Some **4** = Yes **5** = Yes, Very Well

Evaluation of Question # ___
Does the explanation support the answer of true or false?   1 2 3 4 5
Is there good textual evidence to support the answer?   1 2 3 4 5
Is the answer clearly stated?   1 2 3 4 5
        Total Score _____ of a possible 15 points

Evaluation of Question # ___
Does the explanation support the answer of true or false?   1 2 3 4 5
Is there good textual evidence to support the answer?   1 2 3 4 5
Is the answer clearly stated?   1 2 3 4 5
        Total Score _____ of a possible 15 points

Evaluation of Question # ___
Does the explanation support the answer of true or false?   1 2 3 4 5
Is there good textual evidence to support the answer?   1 2 3 4 5
Is the answer clearly stated?   1 2 3 4 5
        Total Score _____ of a possible 15 points

Evaluation of Question # ___
Does the explanation support the answer of true or false?   1 2 3 4 5
Is there good textual evidence to support the answer?   1 2 3 4 5
Is the answer clearly stated?   1 2 3 4 5
        Total Score _____ of a possible 15 points

Evaluation of Question # ___
Does the explanation support the answer of true or false?   1 2 3 4 5
Is there good textual evidence to support the answer?   1 2 3 4 5
Is the answer clearly stated?   1 2 3 4 5
        Total Score _____ of a possible 15 points

Of Mice And Men Overview: True or False?

Write *True* or *False* in the blank next to each statement. Below the statement, explain why you chose true or false, referencing the text to support your choices.

_____ 1. Lennie stole Carlson's gun.

_____ 2. Candy lost his hand in a farming accident.

_____ 3. George almost caused Lennie to drown.

Of Mice And Men Overview True or False? Page 2

_____ 4. Candy is threatened with being lynched.

_____ 5. George admits to himself that he always knew the dream was unattainable.

_____ 6. Slim believes that George's killing of Lennie is irresponsible.

Of Mice And Men Overview: True or False? Suggested Answers

Write *True* or *False* in the blank next to each statement. Below the statement, explain why you chose true or false, referencing the text to support your choices.

FALSE 1. Lennie stole Carlson's gun.

> George steals Carlson's gun, though he misleads the others into believing that Lennie had stolen it. It gave George an "excuse" to overpower Lennie and kill Lennie in purported "self-defense." Lennie is too simpleminded to execute a plan that would involve stealing and using a gun.

TRUE 2. Candy lost his hand in a farming accident.

> As Candy tells about it, his anxiety and discomfort show: "He scratched the stump of his wrist nervously." He tells them that he was injured four years earlier. He believes that he will be fired when he is perceived as no longer useful.

TRUE 3. George almost caused Lennie to drown.

> George explains how Lennie's reaction to his cruel and unthinking prank changed the way he acted toward Lennie: "I was feelin' pretty smart. I turns to Lennie and says, 'Jump in.' An' he jumps. Couldn't swim a stroke. He damn near drowned before we could get him. An' he was so damn nice to me for pullin' him out."

FALSE 4. Candy is threatened with being lynched.

> Curley's wife threatens Crooks: "She turned on him in scorn. "Listen, Nigger," she said. "You know what I can do to you if you open your trap?" As a woman, she does not have a lot of authority to exercise over Candy or Lennie, but as a white woman, she has power over Crooks, a black man.

Of Mice And Men Overview: True or False? Suggested Answers Page 2

TRUE 5. George admits to himself that he always knew the dream was unattainable.

It was Lennie's innocent enthusiasm that made the dream seem palpable for George: "-I think I knowed from the very first. I think I know'd we'd never do her. He usta like to hear about it so much I got to thinking maybe we would."

FALSE 6. Slim believes that George's killing of Lennie is irresponsible.

With Slim as a pseudo-minister and voice of moral authority, he provides George with a sort of simple but profound absolution as he offers him kindness after the lynching party discovers Lennie's body: "A guy got to sometimes."

Of Mice And Men Overview
Reading Activity 2: Analyzing Passages

Anchor Standard	8th Grade	9th-10th Grade
CCRA.R.6	RL.8.1	RL.9-10.1
	RL.8.3	
	RL.8.4	RL.9-10.4
	RL.8.6	
CCRA.SL.1	SL.8.1	SL.9-10.1

Objectives
- Students will analyze what the text says explicitly as well as inferences drawn from the text.
- Students will analyze how different points of view of the characters and the audience (or reader) creates suspense or humor.
- Students will analyze the impact of specific word choices on meaning and tone.

Directions
On the pages that follow, there are 8 passages to analyze, each with a question or questions to guide the process. There are many ways to use these questions:

- You could use them as a worksheet for all students to complete individually.
- You could use the worksheet as your guide in a whole-class discussion. Have students turn to the first passage in the book, read it, then ask the question(s) orally. Repeat through all 8 questions.
- You could assign one passage to each of 8 different groups of students, for the students to discuss and come up with responses to the question(s). Then hold a whole-class discussion.
- You could read the passage and then see which student can find the passage first (to practice skimming skills). Then follow up with the questions(s) and discussion.
- You could have students choose one or two questions to respond to in writing in their notebooks or journals.

Follow-Up/Assessment/Extension
- Ask students to write about the concept of justice. In what ways does justice prevail in the novel, in what ways does justice fail?
- Have students pick out other passages in this chapter that show interesting word usage, descriptions, or lack of clarity.
- As an introduction to this activity, ask students to consider the definition of dreams. Students can answer the question: are dreams meant to come true?

Of Mice And Men Overview Analyzing Passages

Answer the questions following the quotations completely.

1. Evening of a hot day started the little wind to moving among the leaves. The shade climbed up the hills toward the top. On the sand banks the rabbits sat as quietly as little gray sculptured stones. And then from the direction of the state highway came the sound of footsteps on crisp sycamore leaves. The rabbits hurried noiselessly for cover. A stilted heron labored up into the air and pounded down river. For a moment the place was lifeless, and then two men emerged from the path and came into the opening by the green pool.

What do rabbits symbolize?

_____

_____

_____

2. A guy sets alone out here at night, maybe readin' books or thinkin' or stuff like that. Sometimes he gets thinkin', an' he got nothing to tell him what's so an' what ain't so. Maybe if he sees somethin', he don't know whether it's right or not. He can't turn to some other guy and ast him if he sees it too. He can't tell. He got nothing to measure by. I seen things out here. I wasn't drunk. I don't know if I was asleep. If some guy was with me, he could tell me I was asleep, an' then it would be all right. But I jus' don't know.

What does "measure" mean here?

_____

_____

_____

3. George looked around at Lennie. "Jesus, what a tramp," he said. "So that's what Curley picks for a wife." "She's purty," said Lennie defensively. "Yeah, and she's sure hidin' it. Curley got his work ahead of him. Bet she'd clear out for twenty bucks."

Lennie still stared at the doorway where she had been. "Gosh, she was purty." He smiled admiringly.

George looked quickly down at him and then he took him by an ear and shook him. "Listen to me, you crazy bastard," he said fiercely. "Don't you even take a look at that bitch. I don't care what she says and what she does. I seen 'em poison before, but I never seen no piece of jail bait worse than her. You leave her be."

Why is it significant that Curley's wife is never given a name, but referred to by different terms?

_____

_____

_____

Of Mice And Men Overview Analyzing Passages Page 2

4. Crooks reached around and explored his spine with his hand. "I never seen a guy really do it," he said. "I seen guys nearly crazy with loneliness for land, but ever' time a whore house or a blackjack game took what it takes." He hesitated. " . . . . If you . . . . guys would want a hand to work for nothing—just his keep, why I'd come an' lend a hand. I ain't so crippled I can't work like a son-of-a- bitch if I want to."

How are Candy and Crooks similar?

5. Slim twitched George's elbow. "Come on, George. Me an' you'll go in an' get a drink." George let himself be helped to his feet. "Yeah, a drink." Slim said, "You hadda, George. I swear you hadda. Come on with me." He led George into the entrance of the trail and up toward the highway.

How do Slim's actions show his personality?

6. Curley's wife lay with a half-covering of yellow hay. And the meanness and the plannings and the discontent and the ache for attention were all gone from her face. She was very pretty and simple, and her face was sweet and young. Now her rouged cheeks and her reddened lips made her seem alive and sleeping very lightly. The curls, tiny little sausages, were spread on the hay behind her head, and her lips were parted.

In what ways is Curley's wife different in death than in life?

7. "A water snake glided smoothly up the pool, twisting its periscope head from side to side; and it swam the length of the pool and came to the legs of a motionless heron that stood in the shallows. A silent head and beak lanced down and plucked it out by the head, and the beak swallowed the little snake while its tail waved frantically."

What is the significance of the natural world in the novel?

Of Mice And Men Overview Analyzing Passages Suggested Answers

1. Evening of a hot day started the little wind to moving among the leaves. The shade climbed up the hills toward the top. On the sand banks the rabbits sat as quietly as little gray sculptured stones. And then from the direction of the state highway came the sound of footsteps on crisp sycamore leaves. The rabbits hurried noiselessly for cover. A stilted heron labored up into the air and pounded down river. For a moment the place was lifeless, and then two men emerged from the path and came into the opening by the green pool.

What do rabbits symbolize?
The rabbits are emblematic of George and Lennie at the beginning of the novel, but particularly at the end. As the focus of Lennie's dream, the rabbits also represent freedom and autonomy, as they move about at their will. Being weaker and somewhat exposed, the rabbits also represent fear, as they "hurr[y] noiselessly for cover."

2. A guy sets alone out here at night, maybe readin' books or thinkin' or stuff like that. Sometimes he gets thinkin', an' he got nothing to tell him what's so an' what ain't so. Maybe if he sees somethin', he don't know whether it's right or not. He can't turn to some other guy and ast him if he sees it too. He can't tell. He got nothing to measure by. I seen things out here. I wasn't drunk. I don't know if I was asleep. If some guy was with me, he could tell me I was asleep, an' then it would be all right. But I jus' don't know.

What does "measure" mean here?
Crooks is referring to judging one's own mental soundness and sanity by comparing his observations with other people. It speaks to the extreme isolation and loneliness that Crooks experiences. To measure is a comparative relationship, and all Crooks feels is the absence of a standard to measure by, which calls into question for him his own state of mind.

3. George looked around at Lennie. "Jesus, what a tramp," he said. "So that's what Curley picks for a wife." "She's purty," said Lennie defensively. "Yeah, and she's sure hidin' it. Curley got his work ahead of him. Bet she'd clear out for twenty bucks."

Lennie still stared at the doorway where she had been. "Gosh, she was purty." He smiled admiringly.

George looked quickly down at him and then he took him by an ear and shook him. "Listen to me, you crazy bastard," he said fiercely. "Don't you even take a look at that bitch. I don't care what she says and what she does. I seen 'em poison before, but I never seen no piece of jail bait worse than her. You leave her be."

Why is it significant that Curley's wife is never given a name, but referred to by different terms?
She embodies the treatment and role of women in society in general at the time, which is to be unequal to men and to some extent objectified by them. Here she is literally defined by her role in relationship to a man. She does not have her own unique and distinct identity—and whenever she does try to be herself, she is roundly rejected by others—but is "Curley's wife."

4. Crooks reached around and explored his spine with his hand. "I never seen a guy really do it," he said. "I seen guys nearly crazy with loneliness for land, but ever' time a whore house or a blackjack game took what it takes." He hesitated. " . . . . If you . . . . guys would want a hand to work for nothing—just his keep, why I'd come an' lend a hand. I ain't so crippled I can't work like a son-of-a- bitch if I want to."

How are Candy and Crooks similar?
Lennie and Crooks both have a physical disability that makes them more prone than men like Slim or Carlson who are fully able-bodied. This makes the men less secure in their ability to stay employed, which is the only stable area of their lives. This makes them dependent, and it is a major source of anxiety and fear. Crooks and Candy are quick to recognize the independence and self-sufficiency that are at the heart of George and Lennie's dream, and this is why they find it so attractive.

5. Slim twitched George's elbow. "Come on, George. Me an' you'll go in an' get a drink." George let himself be helped to his feet. "Yeah, a drink." Slim said, "You hadda, George. I swear you hadda. Come on with me." He led George into the entrance of the trail and up toward the highway.

How do Slim's actions show his personality?
Slim is a stereotypical alpha-male type character. He is superior to the other men in several ways—his physical body, his degree of handsomeness, his competence at work, and his moral authority. Even in an environment where he is an employee subject to rules, he remains somewhat independent of Curley's machinations. Slim acts on his own accord and with a strong moral compass, and this shows particularly in his intuitive empathy toward George. He acknowledges the difficulty of what George has done, which suggests that Slim is alone among the men in his understanding of the importance of the relationship between George and Lennie.

6. Curley's wife lay with a half-covering of yellow hay. And the meanness and the plannings and the discontent and the ache for attention were all gone from her face. She was very pretty and simple, and her face was sweet and young. Now her rouged cheeks and her reddened lips made her seem alive and sleeping very lightly. The curls, tiny little sausages, were spread on the hay behind her head, and her lips were parted.

In what ways is Curley's wife different in death than in life?
Strangely and shockingly, death transforms her into a character worthy of empathy. She is portrayed as a villain and looming potential threat throughout the novel, but after her accidental death, the unsavory aspects of her character literally disappear ("the meanness and the plannings and the discontent and the ache for attention were all gone from her face"). She appears more "alive" and "sweet" and "young" when she is dead. These inversions of her characterization suggest a decidedly anti-feminist view of women (which may not be Steinbeck's attitude, but a depiction of contemporary views of women).

Of Mice And Men Overview Analyzing Passages Suggested Answers Page 3

7. "A water snake glided smoothly up the pool, twisting its periscope head from side to side; and it swam the length of the pool and came to the legs of a motionless heron that stood in the shallows. A silent head and beak lanced down and plucked it out by the head, and the beak swallowed the little snake while its tail waved frantically."

What is the significance of the natural world in the novel?
The natural world is beautiful and provides a pastoral landscape, but it is filled with remorseless violence, as a matter of fact. The natural world operates according to cycles and hierarchies and the survival of the fittest. Lennie's experience mirrors this, but, among humans, the results are tragic and sad.

Of Mice And Men Overview
Reading Activity 3: Characters, Motivation, and Dreams

Anchor Standard	8th Grade	9th-10th Grade
CCRA.R.1	RL.8.1	RL.9-10.1
CCRA.SL.1	SL.8.1	SL.9-10.1

Objectives
Using textual evidence, students will explore characters' motivations and dreams.

Directions
The Characters, Motivation and Dreams worksheet on the following page could be used in many ways, completed by small groups of students, individual students, or as a whole class activity.

Students will be able to identify how characters' motives create conflict and meaning in the text.

Students may (and should) use their books to skim through the chapters to refresh their memories or gather more information about the characters.

After students complete the worksheets discuss students' answers as a whole class. Collect the worksheets for grading, if you choose, or have students put them in their notebooks for further study.

Follow-Up/Assessment/Extension
Consider what the characters are motivated by and what costs they incur by pursuing their dreams.

Of Mice And Men Overview
Reading Activity 3: Characters, Motivation, and Dreams

Select one of the characters from the list below. Imagine that character at an earlier time in the character's life, sometime before the action of the novel begins.

Candy   Curley   Slim   Carlson   Curley's Wife   Crooks

Step 1: Answer this question: What is this character's main personal dream? To answer the question, think about the character's actions and interests. How could these have fit the goals and ambitions of the character at another point in his or her life?

_____
_____
_____
_____
_____

Step 2: Find a relevant passage in the novel and copy it below. Think about the dream you identified for the character you selected. Is there a point in the novel where we could imagine a flashback when this character's dream is somehow and for some reason revealed?

_____
_____
_____
_____
_____
_____
_____
_____

Of Mice And Men Overview Reading Activity 3: Characters, Motivation, and Dreams Page 2

Step 3: Writing the flashback: On the lines below, write a flashback that is 3 paragraphs long that shows how and why your character believes in their dream. Be descriptive, use dialogue and use details from the novel.

Of Mice And Men Overview Reading Activity 3: Characters, Motivation, and Dreams Suggested Answers

Select one of the characters from the list below. Imagine that character at an earlier time in the character's life, some time before the action of the novel begins.

Candy   Curley   Slim   Carlson   Curley's Wife   Crooks

Step 1: Answer this question: What is this character's main dream for him or herself? To answer the question, think about the character's actions and interests. How could these have fit the goals and ambitions of the character at another point in his or her life?

Here are some ideas:

Candy: His possible main dreams could be to have his health, own his own farm or have a group of close friends.

Curley: His possible main dreams could be becoming a prize-winning boxer, marrying a faithful woman, or taking control over his father's ranch.

Slim: His dream may have been to have a profession where he helps others (sheriff, minister, judge).

Carlson: His dream may be to be a revered and well-respected macho man, not unlike Slim.

Curley's wife: Her dreams may include become a celebrity, being wealthy or enhancing her social status.

Crooks: He may dream about having his family nearby, having a family of his own, having his health or living in a world without prejudice.

Step 2: Find a relevant passage in the novel and copy it below. Think about the dream you identified for the character you selected. Is there a point in the novel where we could imagine a flashback when this character's dream is somehow and for some reason revealed?

Answers will vary.

Step 3: Writing the flashback: On the lines below, write a flashback that is 3 paragraphs long that shows how and why your character believes in their dream. Be descriptive, use dialogue and use details from the novel.

Answers will vary.

Of Mice And Men Overview
Reading Activity 4: Action, Character, Decision

Anchor Standard	8th Grade	9th-10th Grade
CCRA.R.1	RL.8.3	
CCRA.SL.1	SL.8.1	SL.9-10.1

Objective
Students will identify whether particular lines of dialogue or incidents in the story propel the action, reveal aspects of a character, or provoke a decision.

Directions
The following page contains passages chosen from the entirety of Of Mice and Men. Students should determine whether the passages advance the action, reveal aspects of a character, or provoke a decision.

This can be done as a whole-class activity, individually, or in small groups.

Follow-Up/Assessment/Extension
Have students skim the novel to find one example of a passage that propels the action, one that reveals aspects of a character, and one that provokes a decision. Again, this could be done individually or as a group.

Of Mice And Men Overview: Action, Character, Decision

Write **A** (for Action) **C** (for Character) or **D** (for Decision) in the blank next to each to identify whether the passage/statement advances the action, tells us more about a character, or provokes a decision. On the lines under each question, provide a short explanation of your choice.

____ 1. "'Course you did. Well, look. Lennie- if you jus' happen to get in trouble like you always done before, I want you to come right here an' hide in the brush."

____ 2. His arms gradually bent at the elbows and his hands closed into fists. He stiffened and went into a slight crouch. His glance was at once calculating and pugnacious.

____ 3. "Listen to me, you crazy bastard," he said fiercely. "Don't you even take a look at that bitch. I don't care what she says and what she does. I seen 'em poison before, but I never seen no piece of jail bait worse than her. You leave her be."

____ 4. Crooks had reduced himself to nothing. There was no personality, no ego- nothing to arouse either like or dislike.

____ 5. She struggled violently under his hands. Her feet battered on the hay and she writhed to be free; and from under Lennie's hand came a muffled screaming. Lennie began to cry with fright.

Of Mice And Men Overview:
Action, Character, Decision Suggested Answers

Write **A** (for Action) **C** (for Character) or **D** (for Decision) in the blank next to each to identify whether the passage/statement advances the action, tells us more about a character, or provokes a decision. On the lines under each question, provide a short explanation of your choice.

D 1. "'Course you did. Well, look. Lennie- if you jus' happen to get in trouble like you always done before, I want you to come right here an' hide in the brush."
George very deliberately makes a plan for Lennie to follow if problems happen again and drills Lennie to follow this decision.

C 2. His arms gradually bent at the elbows and his hands closed into fists. He stiffened and went into a slight crouch. His glance was at once calculating and pugnacious.
Curley's instinctual response to a casual confrontation reveal his pugilist nature—he immediately falls into a boxing stance. This is Curley's form of problem solving and a major personality defect.

D 3. "Listen to me, you crazy bastard," he said fiercely. "Don't you even take a look at that bitch. I don't care what she says and what she does. I seen 'em poison before, but I never seen no piece of jail bait worse than her. You leave her be."
Again, George makes definitive decisions for Lennie and coaches him to abide by them to avoid entanglements.

C 4. Crooks had reduced himself to nothing. There was no personality, no ego- nothing to arouse either like or dislike.
After a confrontation with Curley's wife in which she "puts him in his place," Crooks is shown to retract into himself and conform to racist expectations for his behavior. It shows how Crooks is broken by racial segregation and how much he longs for connection with others.

A 5. She struggled violently under his hands. Her feet battered on the hay and she writhed to be free; and from under Lennie's hand came a muffled screaming. Lennie began to cry with fright.
The most dramatic incident of the book creates conflict between Lennie and society (as a function of the need for justice) and spurs on actions that result in Lennie's death.

Of Mice And Men Overview
Reading Activity 5: Figurative Language

Anchor Standard	8th Grade	9th-10th Grade
CCRA.R.4	RL.8.4	RL.9-10.4
CCRA.SL.1	SL.8.1	SL.9-10.1

Objectives
- Students will determine the meaning of words and phrases as they are used in the text, and how hyperbole and understatement creates meaning.
- Students will determine how figurative language contributes to meaning.

Directions
The following page has a passage from the text which includes examples of figurative language. This work-sheet can be done individually, as a whole-class activity, or in small groups. Discuss the answers as a whole class. Collect the worksheets and record the grades if you choose to do so.

Follow-Up/Assessment/Extension
Ask students to begin tracking instances of a particular type of figurative language (personification, metaphor, hyperbole, etc.) in the text. Ask students to make a list to track their observations. Assign students a paper that uses these examples to make an argument about how the language creates meaning.

Of Mice And Men Overview: Figurative Language

Read the following passages and determine if the passage contains hyperbole (H) or metaphor (M). On the lines below, explain how figurative language create meaning in the passage.

_____1. Behind him walked his opposite, a huge man, shapeless of face, with large, pale eyes, and wide, sloping shoulders; and he walked heavily, dragging his feet a little, the way a bear drags his paws. His arms did not swing at his sides, but hung loosely.

_____2. He was a jerkline skinner, the prince of the ranch, capable of driving ten, sixteen, even twenty mules with a single line to the leaders.

_____3. 3. You jus' let 'em try to get the rabbits. I'll break their God damn necks. I'll . . . . I'll smash 'em with a stick." He subsided, grumbling to himself, threatening the future cats which might dare to disturb the future rabbits.

_____4. Crooks bored in on him. "Want me ta tell ya what'll happen? They'll take ya to the booby hatch. They'll tie ya up with a collar, like a dog."

Of Mice And Men Overview: Figurative Language Suggested Answers

Read the following passages and determine if the passage contains hyperbole (H) or metaphor (M). On the lines below, explain how figurative language create meaning in the passage.

M 1. Behind him walked his opposite, a huge man, shapeless of face, with large, pale eyes, and wide, sloping shoulders; and he walked heavily, dragging his feet a little, the way a bear drags his paws. His arms did not swing at his sides, but hung loosely.
This quote is a metaphor because it described this man (Lennie) as if he is a bear, but does not set his description up in comparison to a bear.

M 2. He was a jerkline skinner, the prince of the ranch, capable of driving ten, sixteen, even twenty mules with a single line to the leaders.
This passage contains a metaphor because it speaks of Slim as if he were actually a prince. This metaphor serves to make the reader feel the regal and important way in which Slim carries himself, and therefore the way others see him.

H 3. You jus' let 'em try to get the rabbits. I'll break their God damn necks. I'll . . . . I'll smash 'em with a stick." He subsided, grumbling to himself, threatening the future cats which might dare to disturb the future rabbits.
Lennie is so excited about his dream that he defends it against any encroachment—here he exaggerates (one hopes) the physical force he would use against cats that might harm his rabbits.

H 4. Crooks bored in on him. "Want me ta tell ya what'll happen? They'll take ya to the booby hatch. They'll tie ya up with a collar, like a dog."
Crooks is deliberately being cruel. He hyperbolizes purposefully to upset Lennie.

Of Mice And Men Novel Overview
Reading Activity 6: Elements of Fiction & Literary Devices

Objective
Students will study and discuss passages from the text to examine foreshadowing, suspense, conflict and plot.

Directions
Use the following passages and discussion questions as a guide to discussing key elements of fiction and literary devices in this chapters. You can give students the questions ahead of time and have them formulate answers prior to the class discussion or you can jump right in with a whole class discussion without student preparation if your students will handle that well.

As you hold the class discussion, be sure to include conversations defining foreshadowing, suspense, conflict and plot.

Follow-Up/Assessment/Extension
After your discussion, ask students to look for these elements throughout the novel.

Of Mice And Men Overview: Elements of Fiction & Literary Devices

Explain how the following foreshadow future events in the novel.

1. Lennie's petting dead mice

2. The incident in Weed

3. George's escape plan

4. The death of Candy's dog.

5. Lennie's breaking Curley's hand

6. Lennie's being fascinated by Curley's wife

7. The death of Lennie's puppy

Of Mice And Men Overview:
Elements of Fiction & Literary Devices Suggested Answers

Explain how the following foreshadow future events in the **novel.**

1. Lennie's petting dead mice
   Despite George's exhortations that the dead mice "ain't fresh" and should be discarded, Lennie cannot help but indulge in his impulsive whim to pet something soft. This is especially seen as he is deceitful and says he discarded the corpse when he did not. Later in the novel Lennie will also have difficulty managing his obsessive fixation and impulsivity when petting the puppy and when touching Curley's wife's hair.

2. The incident in Weed
   This incident is one primarily of misunderstanding. The situation escalated because Lennie himself was so panicked with fear, which resulted in his holding on more tightly to the woman who felt that she had been assaulted. This is seen again in Lennie's encounter with Curley (hand) and with Curley's wife (resulting in her death).

3. George's escape plan
   Instinctively George knows that an incident will happen again, and that Lennie needs to be protected. Ultimately George is correct. The incident with Curley's wife is foreshadowed.

4. The death of Candy's dog
   Candy expresses regret for not killing the dog himself, which would have been a show of loyalty to a long valued pet companion. George ultimately acts toward Lennie in this way, offering a compassionate death as an alternative to violent suffering.

5. Lennie's breaking Curley's hand
   This is another step in the escalation toward the accident which breaks Curley's wife's neck and takes her life. This incident conveys that Lennie is unusually strong, and that he is not completely capable of managing his might safely.

6. Lennie's being fascinated by Curley's wife
   While Candy, Crooks, and George look at Lennie with scorn, Lennie literally cannot take his eyes off of her. With her elaborate and colorful clothes and shoes, she represents a variety of textures that Lennie would like to touch. We can see that Lennie's fascination with Curley's wife will lead to trouble.

7. The death of Lennie's puppy
   Lennie accidentally kills the puppy, which foreshadows Lennie's accidently breaking Curley's wife's neck.

Of Mice and Men Novel Overview
Reading Activity 7: Meaning and Inferences

Anchor Standard	8th Grade	9th-10th Grade
CCRA.R.1	RL.8.1	RL.9-10.1
CCRA.SL.1	SL.8.1	SL.9-10.1

Objective
Students will answer questions about selected passages from the text which require them to extract meaning or inferences from the text.

Directions
The following pages contain passages from Novel Overview of *Of Mice and Men* and questions related to the passages that require close reading to answer. Students should answer the questions related to the passages.

This can be done as a whole-class activity, individually, or in small groups. If it is done individually or in small groups, come together as a class to discuss the answers to the questions.

Follow-Up/Assessment/Extension
Collect the worksheets for review and/or grading.

Of Mice And Men Overview: Meaning & Inferences 1

Read the passages and answer the related questions.

1. *George put his hand on Lennie's shoulder. "I ain't takin' it away jus' for meanness. That mouse ain't fresh, Lennie; and besides, you've broke it pettin' it. You get another mouse that's fresh and I'll let you keep it a little while."*

   What doesn't Lennie understand about keeping the mouse?

2. *Slim looked through George and beyond him. "Ain't many guys travel around together," he mused. "I don't know why. Maybe ever'body in the whole damn world is scared of each other."*

   What is Slim suggesting about "guys"? Why is "ever'body" significant?

3. *"You seen what they done to my dog tonight? They says he wasn't no good to himself nor nobody else. When they can me here I wisht somebody'd shoot me. But they won't do nothing like that. I won't have no place to go, an' I can't get no more jobs.*

   In what ways is Candy identifying with his dog?

4. "'Member what I said about hoein' and doin' odd jobs?"
"Yeah," said Candy. "I remember."
"Well, jus' forget it," said Crooks. "I didn't mean it. Jus' foolin'. I wouldn' want to go no place like that."

How does Crooks's changing his mind relate to fear?

5. *He moved his hand a little and her hoarse cry came out. Then Lennie grew angry. "Now don't," he said. "I don't want you to yell. You gonna get me in trouble jus' like George says you will. Now don't you do that." And she continued to struggle, and her eyes were wild with terror. He shook her then, and he was angry with her. "Don't you go yellin'," he said, and he shook her; and her body flopped like a fish. And then she was still, for Lennie had broken her neck.*

Compare this passage to the description of Curley's fight with Lennie. What do they share in common? Why is this significant?

Of Mice And Men Overview: Meaning & Inferences 1 Suggested Answers

Read the passages and answer the related questions.

1. *George put his hand on Lennie's shoulder. "I ain't takin' it away jus' for meanness. That mouse ain't fresh, Lennie; and besides, you've broke it pettin' it. You get another mouse that's fresh and I'll let you keep it a little while."*

What doesn't Lennie understand about keeping the mouse?
Lennie does not understand the reason that it is bad for him to keep the mouse. For him, the dead mouse is merely a soft thing to pet and comfort him; he does not care that the mouse is dead; it's still soft and comforting in his pocket.

2. *Slim looked through George and beyond him. "Ain't many guys travel around together," he mused. "I don't know why. Maybe ever'body in the whole damn world is scared of each other."*

What is Slim suggesting about "guys"? Why is "ever'body" significant?
Slim is suggesting that "guys" keep to themselves and don't pair up or rely on other people like George and Lennie do because they are afraid of everyone else. It is significant that Slim says "ever'body" is like this because it shows just how different George and Lennie are for relying on each other.

3. *"You seen what they done to my dog tonight? They says he wasn't no good to himself nor nobody else. When they can me here I wisht somebody'd shoot me. But they won't do nothing like that. I won't have no place to go, an' I can't get no more jobs.*

In what ways is Candy identifying with his dog?
He recognizes that when he is no longer useful, that he is disposable, just as Carlson felt the dog was.

4. "'Member what I said about hoein' and doin' odd jobs?"
"Yeah," said Candy. "I remember."
"Well, jus' forget it," said Crooks. "I didn't mean it. Jus' foolin'. I wouldn' want to go no place like that."

How does Crooks's changing his mind relate to fear?
The word "forget" is used several times in the chapter, particularly when Candy and Lennie's presence in Crooks's room make Crooks "forget" about the way he is treated by society because of his race. Crooks is reminded that unjust, unfair, arbitrary claims from a white woman can literally end his life, and he is scared back into submission, giving up on the farm dream.

Of Mice And Men Overview: Meaning & Inferences 1 Suggested Answers Page 2

5. *He moved his hand a little and her hoarse cry came out. Then Lennie grew angry. "Now don't," he said. "I don't want you to yell. You gonna get me in trouble jus' like George says you will. Now don't you do that." And she continued to struggle, and her eyes were wild with terror. He shook her then, and he was angry with her. "Don't you go yellin'," he said, and he shook her; and her body flopped like a fish. And then she was still, for Lennie had broken her neck.*

Compare this passage to the description of Curley's fight with Lennie. What do they share in common? Why is this significant?

In both passages, Lennie's "victims" are described as fish. This connects the people to the natural world that Steinbeck describes in the Salinas Valley. Just as Curley and his wife are "fish," Lennie is often characterized as bear-like, a natural predator of fish. When bears kill fish, it is part of the natural cycle—it is not exactly murder, just as Lennie's incidents of violence are not malicious. It characterizes Lennie as innocent in an animal-like way.

Of Mice And Men Overview: Meaning & Inferences 2

Read the passage and answer the related questions.

Guys like us, that work on ranches, are the loneliest guys in the world. They got no family. They don't belong no place. . . . With us it ain't like that. We got a future. We got somebody to talk to that gives a damn about us. We don't have to sit in no bar room blowin' in our jack jus' because we got no place else to go. If them other guys gets in jail they can rot for all anybody gives a damn. But not us.

1. What is the effect of the excessive use of pronouns in this passage?

2. Why, according to George, do most ranchers participate in counterproductive behaviors?

3. What is the cost of being isolated? What is the benefit of being together?

Of Mice And Men Overview: Meaning & Inferences 2 Suggested Answers

Read the passage and answer the related questions.

Guys like us, that work on ranches, are the loneliest guys in the world. They got no family. They don't belong no place. . . . With us it ain't like that. We got a future. We got somebody to talk to that gives a damn about us. We don't have to sit in no bar room blowin' in our jack jus' because we got no place else to go. If them other guys gets in jail they can rot for all anybody gives a damn. But not us.

1. What is the effect of the excessive use of pronouns in this passage?
The emphasis on pronouns sets up a dichotomy of us versus them, making the "us" a far more preferable circumstance.

2. Why, according to George, do most ranchers participate in counterproductive behaviors?
Interestingly, it does not have to do with caring for another person, but instead with being cared for ("gives a damn about us" and "for all anybody gives a damn"). It is through the care of someone else that a rancher can make a more constructive decision to live better.

3. What is the cost of being isolated? What is the benefit of being together?
The cost of isolation is not belonging and not having a future. Being together creates a more deliberate life which is focused on the attainment of shared goals, as opposed to immediate, hedonistic pleasures.

Of Mice and Men Novel Overview
Writing Activity 1: Sharing a Common Dream

Anchor Standard	8th Grade	9th-10th Grade
CCRA.SL.1	SL.8.1, 1a-1d	SL.9-10.1, 1a-1d
CCRA.SL.3	SL.8.4	SL.9-10.4
CCRA.W.1	W.8.2	W.9-10.2
CCRA.W.2	W.8.4	W.9-10.4
CCRA.W.4	W.8.5	W.9-10.5
CCRA.W.5		W.9-10.7
		W.9-10.9, 9b

Objectives
- Students will evaluate and analyze textual evidence to explore the isolation.
- Students will evaluate passages that reveal characterization, motive and conflict caused by society.
- Students will examine language for ways in which characterization, motive and conflict illuminate the definitions of weakness and strength presented in the novel.
- Students will write a composition in which they consider their analysis of relevant passages to answer the question, "Is sharing a common dream possible?"

Directions
The following series of worksheets and information organizers can be used by students individually, in small groups, or done partly as a whole-class activity. They are intended to guide students through the process of reading and thinking critically about information by ultimately answering the single question, "Is sharing a common dream possible?"

Preview the following pages. Determine the best way to have your particular class handle this assignment (individually, pairs, groups, whole-class, or some combination). A combination of group work (to do the analyzing of the text on the chart page) followed by individual work (to do the second and third pages of the assignment) would most likely be best to fulfill the standards listed for this assignment.

Follow-Up/Assessment/Extension
- The written assignment will be a good basis for assessment of the students' success with this assignment. Create a rubric explaining the criteria on which their written assignments will be evaluated.
- Tell students to continue observing examples of how weakness and strength are depicted in the novel. Consider how these relate to race, gender and social position.
- Have some students read/present their writing assignments to the class to practice more speaking/listening skills and to expose all students to each others' ideas.

Of Mice And Men Overview: "Is Sharing A Common Dream Possible?"

One of the central themes in *Of Mice and Men* is that many of the characters are working to unite with one another. They share a collective dream and are working to realize that dream. However, there are forces at work that divide them and keep them from achieving this dream. Write a paper in which you (a) characterize their common dream and (b) explain at least two forces that keep this dream from becoming a reality.

To explore the idea of sharing a common dream:

1. Identify passages and quotes about the characters who have shared dreams.

2. Examine the context of your quotes.

3. Consider the connotation and denotation of key phrases in your quotes.
    a. What is the tone?
    b. Is there a conflict?
    c. What forces keep characters from uniting?
    d. Can those forces realistically be overcome?

4. Look for patterns in your evidence. Is a word or idea repeated? Use these patterns to shape an answer to the question.

Of Mice And Men Overview: "Is Sharing A Common Dream Possible?" Page 2

Complete the chart to analyze information to develop ideas to write your essay.

Describe the dream	Who believes in the dream?	What obstacles do they face in achieving their dream?	Can the obstacles be overcome? How or why not?

Of Mice And Men Overview: "Is Sharing A Common Dream Possible?" Page 3

Evaluate Your Textual Evidence

1. What societal beliefs hold the characters back from achieving their dreams?

2. How do the characters feel about these societal beliefs?

3. What motivates the characters?

Of Mice And Men Overview
Suggested Writing Assignments

Anchor Standard	8th Grade	9th-10th Grade
CCRA.W.1	W.8.1, 1a-1d	W.9-10.1, 1a-1e
CCRA.W.2	W.8.2, 2a-2f	W.9-10.2, 2a-2f
CCRA.W.3	W.8.3, 3a-3e	W.9-10.3, 3a-3e
CCRA.W.4	W.8.4	W.9-10.4
CCRA.W.5	W.8.5	W.9-10.5

Objective
Students will be assigned or will choose one of a selection of writing assignments pertaining to Novel Overview of *Of Mice and Men* to fulfill one or more of the standards listed above.

Directions
To provide you with maximum flexibility for differentiated instruction, the following page has a list of suggested writing assignments, all related to Novel Overview of *Of Mice and Men*. Either assign individual students particular assignments to do or allow students to choose their own assignments.

A second page of "Quick Write" topics is also included.

Follow-Up/Assessment/Extension
- Have dramatic readings of students' narratives or poems.
- Create a "reading room" space in your classroom where students can donate their writing assignments for others in the class to read.
- Allow students to do more than one assignment if they want to.
- Use the "left-over" assignments (not chosen for this activity) as topics for journal entries.

Of Mice and Men Novel Overview: Creative Analytical Writing Assignments

1. Write the story of Candy's dog, recalling its vitality and youth.
2. What is George thinking as he shoots Lennie?
3. Will Lennie and Slim become friends?
4. Write a narrative description of Candy shooting the dog.
5. Does Curley believe that justice was served?
6. Write a description of the ranch from Curley's wife's perspective.
7. Define friendship.
8. Write a newspaper article about Lennie's death.
9. Write the final scene from a different character's perspective (Slim, Carlson or Curley).
10. Write a eulogy for Lennie from George's perspective.

Of Mice and Men Novel Overview: Quick-Write Writing Assignments

1. Is George responsible for Lennie?
2. Is Lennie "nuts"?
3. Is Curley's wife misunderstood?
4. Which character is most mistreated? Why?
5. Why is it significant that George mentions his "stake" so many times?
6. Why does Slim have so much moral authority?
7. Could Crooks be less isolated?
8. What roles does prejudice play in the novel?
9. How is farming a form of domestication? Are mice, puppies and rabbits domesticated?
10. Are the foreshadows too literal?